BOY SCOUTS OF AMERICA
MERIT BADGE SERIES

PUBLIC HEALTH

DEC 10 2010
FARMINGTON COMMUNITY LIBRARY
FARMINGTON HILLS BRANCH
32737 WEST TWELVE MILE ROAD
FARMINGTON HILLS, MI 48334-3302
(248) 553-0300

Requirements

1. Explain what public health is. Explain how *Escherichia coli (E. coli)*, tetanus, AIDS, encephalitis, salmonellosis, and Lyme disease are contracted. Then, pick any four of the following diseases and explain how each one is contracted: gonorrhea, West Nile virus, botulism, influenza, syphilis, hepatitis, emphysema, meningitis, herpes, lead poisoning. For all 10 diseases, explain the type or form of the disease (viral, bacterial, environmental, toxin), any possible vectors for transmission, ways to help prevent the spread of infection, and available treatments.

2. Do the following:

    a. Explain the meaning of *immunization.*

    b. Name five diseases against which a young child should be immunized and two diseases against which everyone should be reimmunized periodically.

    c. Using the diseases you chose for requirement 1, discuss the diseases for which there is currently no treatment or immunization.

3. Discuss the importance of safe drinking water in terms of the spread of disease. Then, demonstrate two ways for making water safe to drink that can be used while at camp. In your demonstration, explain how dishes and utensils should be washed, dried, and kept sanitary at home and in camp.

4. Explain what a vector is and how insects and rodents can be controlled in your home, in your community, and at camp. Tell why this is important. In your discussion, explain which vectors can be easily controlled by individuals and which ones require long-term, collective action.

5. With your parent's and counselor's approval, do ONE of the following:

   a. Visit a municipal wastewater treatment facility OR a solid-waste management operation in your community. Describe how the facility safely treats and disposes of sewage or solid waste. Describe how sewage and solid waste should be disposed of under wilderness camping conditions.

   b. Arrange to meet with the food service manager of a food service facility (such as a restaurant or school cafeteria) and visit this establishment. Observe food preparation, handling, and storage, and learn how the facility keeps foods from becoming contaminated. Find out what conditions allow microorganisms to multiply in food and how conditions can be controlled to help prevent the growth and dissemination of microorganisms. Learn how microorganisms in food can be killed. Discuss what you learned with your counselor.

6. Do the following:

   a. Describe the health dangers from air, water, and noise pollution.

   b. Describe health dangers from tobacco use and alcohol and drug abuse.

7. With your parent's and counselor's approval, visit your city, county, or state public health agency. Discuss how the agency addresses the concerns raised in requirements 1 through 6 and how the services provided by this agency affect your family. Then do the following:

   a. Compare the four leading causes of mortality (death) in your community for any of the past five years with the four leading causes of morbidity (incidence of disease) in your community. Explain how the public health agency you visited is trying to reduce the mortality and morbidity rates of these leading causes of illness and death.

b. Explain the role of the health agency you visited related to the outbreak of diseases.

c. Discuss the kinds of public assistance the agency is able to provide in case of disasters such as floods, storms, tornadoes, earthquakes, and other acts of destruction. Your discussion can include the cleanup necessary after a disaster occurs.

8. Pick a profession in the public health sector that interests you. Find out the education, training, and experience required to work in this profession. Discuss what you learn with your counselor.

Contents

Introduction 7
Diseases 17
Food Sanitation 41
Sanitation in the Community and at Camp 47
Pollution and Health 61
Tobacco, Alcohol, and Drugs 69
Careers in Public Health 75
Resources 78

Introduction

The field of public health deals with maintaining and monitoring the health of communities, and with the detection, cure, and prevention of health risks and diseases. Although public health is generally seen as a community-oriented service, it actually starts with the individual. From a single individual to the family unit to the smallest isolated rural town to the worldwide global community, one person can influence the health of many.

> The public health team is made up of all sorts of members working at all levels of health care. For example, a private-practice doctor might treat a patient for food poisoning that turns out to be salmonellosis. The doctor reports this case to the local health department, which gathers this information. From there, local or state public health officials might be called to investigate multiple reports of food poisoning in the area, locate the source of the salmonellosis, and initiate prevention and containment programs to help prevent others from contracting salmonellosis.

As you work on the Public Health merit badge, remember that public health begins with the individual—with you—and from there grows out into the community, and into the whole world. What you learn in earning this merit badge can be of as much value to you and your own personal health as it is to your entire community.

INTRODUCTION

Public Health Goals

The four main goals of public health are

- To help prevent disease and injury
- To teach people how to be healthy
- To provide basic health services to certain communities
- To help protect people from environmental hazards such as pollution

> Public health officials work to prevent disease by attacking the sources of diseases. When efforts to prevent a disease fail, health workers try to contain the source of a disease or an outbreak of illness.

As you can see, the goals of public health cover many different types of health issues. Because of this, many types of public health specialists with different responsibilities work together to try to meet these goals.

Local health *inspectors* make sure that health codes and regulations are being followed. They may drop by restaurants to ensure that foods are stored at the right temperature, dishes are washed properly, and the people handling food are following food-safety rules. Other kinds of inspectors will check a city's drinking water for dangerous levels of contaminants such as lead and arsenic or bacteria.

Health inspectors enforce laws that help ensure the public's well-being.

INTRODUCTION

Many public health scientists investigate and research the sometimes mysterious causes of illnesses. These are the detectives of the public health world, and they are called *epidemiologists.* For example, after an outbreak of a deadly respiratory disease in 1993 in the southwest United States, public health scientists determined the cause to be a hantavirus spread by rodent droppings. When there is an outbreak of food poisoning, public health scientists try to track down the source, such as a supply of hamburger meat infected with the bacterium *Escherichia coli.*

Doctors and nurses are often public health workers, especially those who work at community clinics or travel to serve remote communities. Many people live far away from hospitals and doctors' offices. The traveling medical units of public health agencies help these people to get the medicines and checkups they need.

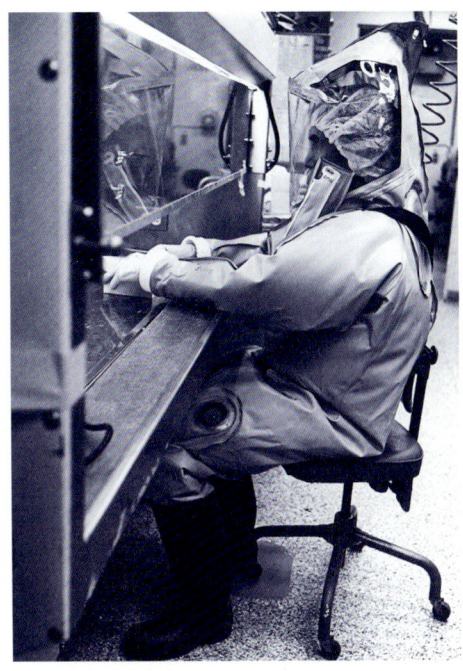

The federal and state governments employ many kinds of public health workers, like this lab technician.

An *epidemic* is an outbreak, or sudden increase, of a disease that spreads quickly and widely, infecting many people at the same time. You probably have heard of or even experienced a flu epidemic. *Epidemiology* is the medical science that studies the occurrence and spread of diseases in large populations.

PUBLIC HEALTH 9

INTRODUCTION

Dentists and veterinarians are part of the public health realm, too. Dental health is vital to any individual's well-being, and rabies (among other veterinary-related diseases) also is a public health concern.

Some members of the public health community are educators. They may visit individual families, schools, and workplaces to teach people about the hazards they might encounter at home, in the community, or at work. For instance, educators could visit factories to warn people who work in loud conditions that noise eventually will cause permanent damage to their hearing. The educators might hand out pamphlets encouraging employees to wear the protective gear their employer provides.

> *Statisticians* keep records about the occurrence of diseases, injuries, and other threats to public health, often helping to develop new laws and regulations that help control public health risks. They provide reports that help communities predict such things as when to spray for mosquitoes or offer an immunization program.

National Health Services

In the United States, the Department of Health and Human Services oversees many of the efforts to protect public health. The head of the department—the secretary of Health and Human Services—is appointed by the president of the United States.

The HHS is made up of many large departments that specialize in various areas of public health. For example, the **Food and Drug Administration** ensures that *pharmaceuticals* (drugs), cosmetics, and food are safe for our use and consumption. The FDA tests drugs before they are put on the market, and approves and licenses them for human consumption and for sale. The FDA issues *consumer alerts* that warn people about things that might pose a risk to someone, such as tobacco products or some food additives, or maybe even trace amounts of peanut oil in a plain brownie mix. An alert like this could save the life of someone who is highly allergic to peanuts. The FDA also can prohibit the sale of a food or drug that it decides is too dangerous.

Another federal agency involved in public health is the **National Institutes of Health,** which conducts research in its own laboratories. It also helps other organizations, such as universities, hospitals, and medical schools, that are trying to prevent and cure illnesses all over the world. One way the NIH supports research is by maintaining the National Library of Medicine—the largest research library of health sciences in the world. This library is an important source of information for scientists, doctors, and statisticians.

The **Centers for Disease Control and Prevention** researches diseases, keeps track of statistics about diseases, and works to prevent the spread of disease. Together with state, county, and city health departments, the CDC provides immunizations, monitors the safety of drinking water, and investigates outbreaks of disease. Inside the CDC are many organizations that specialize in different areas of public health, such as birth defects, workplace safety, and infectious diseases.

> The CDC's Web site, *http://www.cdc.gov,* is full of information about hundreds of issues, including travelers' health, nutrition, and fighting the flu.

Other federal government departments that are not under the HHS also assist in public health efforts. For example, the **Environmental Protection Agency** investigates and regulates pollution. It might enforce regulations that limit the amount of chemicals a factory can discharge into a river or the air.

Introduction

> The **Public Health Service Commissioned Corps** is another significant branch of the HHS. According to its Web site (see the resources section), this unique agency has programs that
>
> - Provide health care and related services to medically underserved populations.
> - Prevent and control disease, and identify and help correct health hazards in the environment.
> - Promote healthy lifestyles.
> - Ensure the safety and effectiveness of drugs and medical devices, and the safety of food, cosmetics, and electronic products.
> - Conduct and support biomedical, behavioral, and health services research, and assist in the dissemination of the research results to health-care professionals and the public.
> - Work with other countries and international agencies on global health problems and their solutions.
>
> A uniformed service of the United States that is led by the U.S. Surgeon General, the PHS Commissioned Corps is a specialized career = system "designed to attract, develop, and retain health professionals who may be assigned to federal, state, or local agencies or international organizations to accomplish its mission." This agency furnishes health expertise "in time of war or other national or international emergencies."

State, City, and Local Health Services

Local health agencies provide many public health services, some required by federal or state law. They provide drug rehabilitation programs and educate citizens about violence and injury prevention. Many local health departments also sponsor health clinics. Well-baby clinics promote good health in infants, while immunization or screening clinics stress disease prevention. Other clinics may promote dental health or general health. Such agencies often provide rabies control programs, too. They also keep vital statistics about births, deaths, and marriages and the incidence of disease in a community.

Every local health department has an office that handles records of reportable diseases. A *reportable disease*—such as gonorrhea, Lyme disease, or influenza—is one that health officials and doctors are required to report to the local or state health department. When doctors report these cases, the identity of the infected person remains confidential. The local health department summarizes the number of cases and reports these findings to the state health department, which in turn notifies the federal government at the CDC.

Morbidity is the incidence of disease in a population. *Mortality* is the rate of deaths in a population. Both usually are expressed as the number of incidents per 1,000 in a year.

Zoonotic diseases—diseases that affect both humans and animals—such as rabies, must be reported by veterinarians to local or state health departments.

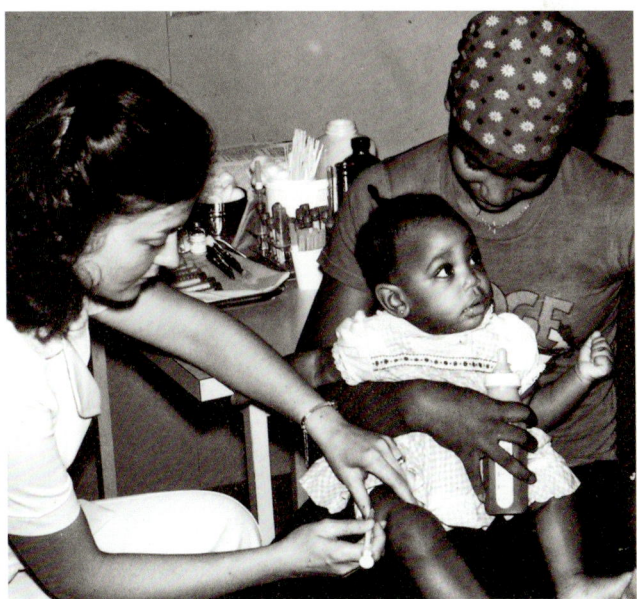

Health clinics run by local physicians, dentists, and nurses, and public health rabies clinics run by veterinarians, usually are open to everybody.

INTRODUCTION

> A division of environmental health within the local department of health, or a department of public works, typically supervises a city's water and sanitation services. Services include delivering clean, *potable* (drinkable) water to homes; processing sewage and other household wastes; and disposing of solid wastes. This department might help to control pests that can carry diseases or endanger public health. Department employees might also inspect public swimming pools, local lakes, and waterfronts to ensure that the water is safe for swimming.

When a disaster such as a flood or earthquake strikes, public health departments help the community in many ways. If a hospital is flooded, public health workers may help move patients of that hospital to a nearby facility. Public health departments may also issue press releases to the media to help citizens know when it is safe to return home. Information may include tips about avoiding floodwater, which may carry disease, or staying clear of fallen power lines, which can be deadly. Public health workers might hand out clean drinking water or set up field medical units to help injured people.

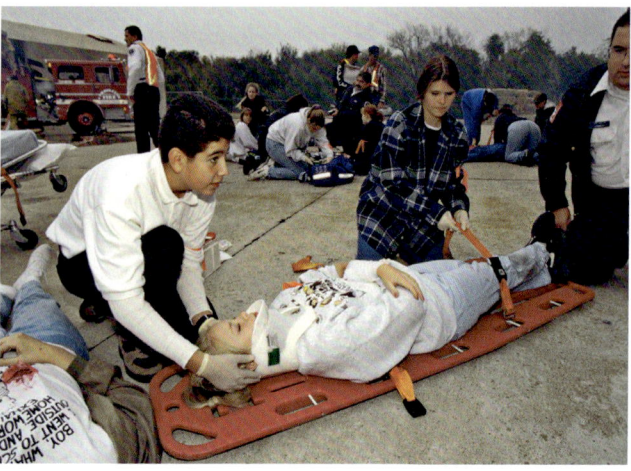

14   PUBLIC HEALTH

Private Health Services

Some agencies that promote public health are supported by private funds and donations. Private agencies typically focus on a single problem area, help people affected by the problem, and sponsor research that might solve the problem. The **National Society for the Prevention of Blindness** is an example.

Public and private agencies may concentrate on the same problem and work together to seek solutions. For example, understanding the processes that start and promote cancer is important to both the **National Cancer Institute** (a federal agency) and the **American Cancer Society** (a private organization). Both agencies sponsor cancer research, seeking better methods for detecting and treating cancer.

Protecting the public health is everyone's responsibility. Each one of us can help ensure everyone else's health and safety by not polluting the air, water, or environment. Individuals also can help by maintaining healthy lifestyles. Communities can help by keeping streets and municipal properties clean and free of litter and by providing a pure water supply and sanitary waste disposal systems.

Adult specimen of a pork tapeworm, taken from the intestine of a human

Diseases

The threat of widespread disease is a major public health issue. Thus one of the responsibilities of public health professionals is to become familiar with diseases, their causes, and their cures to help protect the public from those diseases. But individuals also can help maintain public health, and their own health, by learning about diseases.

> Factors such as the natural spread and transmission of diseases, overcrowding in many underdeveloped countries, the ease of world travel, and the potential spreading of exotic diseases through warfare all make the responsibilities of today's public health officials more and more challenging.

Causes of Disease

Many diseases are caused by bacteria, viruses, parasitic worms, protozoa, fungi, and other *pathogens,* or disease-causing organisms that invade the body. Some examples of these *infectious diseases* are tetanus (bacterial), influenza (viral), athlete's foot (fungal), and hookworm (parasitic).

Other diseases are caused by the *environment*. For example, overexposure to the mineral lead can cause mental impairment and death. Benzene, a chemical found in tobacco smoke, vehicle exhaust, detergents, and other sources, can cause leukemia.

Diseases that are passed through the genes, from parents to offspring, are known as *hereditary* diseases. Examples include sickle-cell anemia and hemophilia.

Still other diseases may be caused by *malnutrition* (unbalanced or inadequate diet), or by *accidents* and injuries, some of which may be associated with cultural practices.

We call diseases *communicable* if they can be communicated, or spread, from one person to another. We call diseases *zoonotic* if they can be transmitted from human to animal or from animal to human.

PUBLIC HEALTH 17

DISEASES

Immunizations, or *vaccines,* offer protection against many infectious diseases.

Prevention, Treatments, and Cures

Of course, preventing a disease in the first place is the best way to combat disease. But after a person has become sick, the goal of health professionals is treatment.

Many types of treatment have been developed for battling pathogens in the body. Some medicines can kill or inhibit certain pathogens, thereby curing the disease. For example, antibiotics can eliminate *H. pylori,* the bacterium that causes most stomach ulcers.

However, some bacteria and viruses have become resistant to the drugs usually used for treatment. The diseases caused by such drug-resistant pathogens are becoming increasingly difficult to cure. Tuberculosis was almost eradicated, but new strains of it are causing worldwide epidemics.

Many diseases, such as AIDS and arthritis, have no medicinal cure. However, medicines and therapies can offer a great deal of help with these diseases. A person with emphysema, for instance, often benefits from breathing exercises and drugs that help dilate (open up) air passages. Physical therapy and drugs that help reduce inflammation in the body (anti-inflammatory medicines) also help people with arthritis.

Antibodies and Immunizations

In most cases, when the body is infected with a disease, it responds naturally (with help from its *immune system*) by making special substances called *antibodies* that fight the pathogen causing the disease. Often, a person's body can cure itself of a disease, such as a cold or the flu, because antibodies have been hard at work.

Antibodies play an important role in *immunization* (also known as *inoculation* or *vaccination*). A vaccine can be made of live pathogens that are greatly weakened in a laboratory. These altered pathogens do not cause serious illness but will help the body to produce antibodies. A vaccine also can be made of killed pathogens or of related organisms that cause a similar but milder disease, or of parts of the pathogen that do not cause the disease but can make the body's immune system respond as if the disease were present. Immunization with a vaccine can give immunity to some diseases.

= Diseases

> Immunization is one of the best ways to protect health and help us avoid infectious diseases.

The idea of vaccination is not new. People have long noticed that individuals who survive a certain disease rarely get the disease a second time. Edward Jenner (1749–1823), an English physician, created the first modern immunization program. Dr. Jenner ground up scabs from people infected with cowpox and poked this material under the skin of others. The people he treated got mild cases of cowpox and became immune to the closely related smallpox virus, a deadly disease at the time. Before immunization became available, one-third to one-half of all smallpox victims died. The survivors usually were badly scarred. Today, through a public health–sponsored international immunization program, smallpox has been virtually eradicated all over the world.

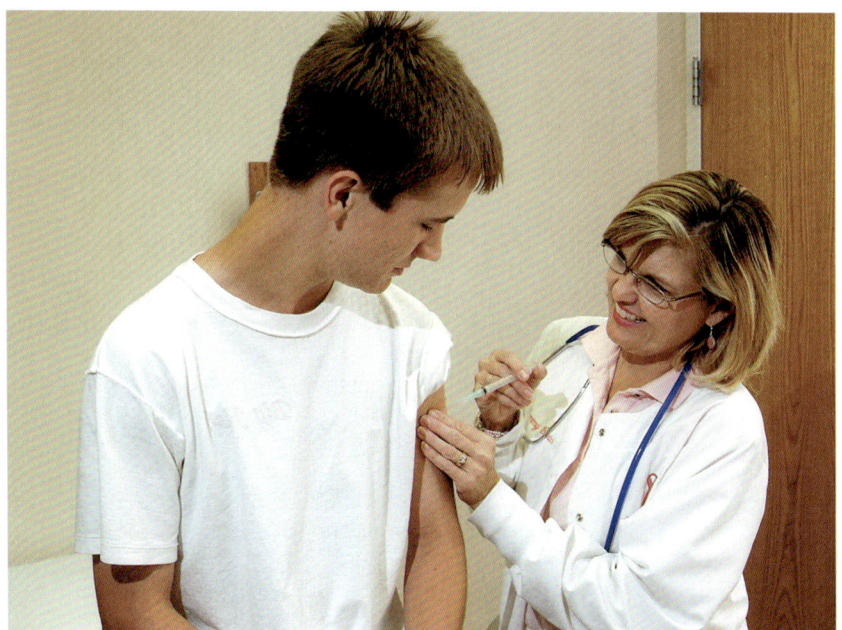

Regular checkups help ensure you stay on track with the recommended vaccine schedule.

PUBLIC HEALTH

Diseases

The immune system makes antibodies for each particular disease that it meets. Therefore, a different vaccine is needed for each disease. Immunization is available today against many diseases found in the United States, including diphthria, pertussis (whooping cough), tetanus, polio, mumps, red mesles (rubeola), German measles (rubella), certain strains of influenza, hepatitis A and B, and chicken pox. Immunizations also are available for many other diseases that are uncommon in the United States but common in other parts of the world, such as yellow fever and typhoid fever. Americans typically receive these immunizations when they travel out of the country or join the armed forces.

Immunization is suggested for very young children, with periodic booster injections as recommended. Antibodies are long-lasting, but the protection they give may decrease with time. A second exposure to a pathogen will increase the level of antibodies a person's body will produce. So a second injection, or *booster shot*, often is given to help strengthen immunity.

> Adults need immunizations, too. For example, tetanus boosters need to be given every 10 years.

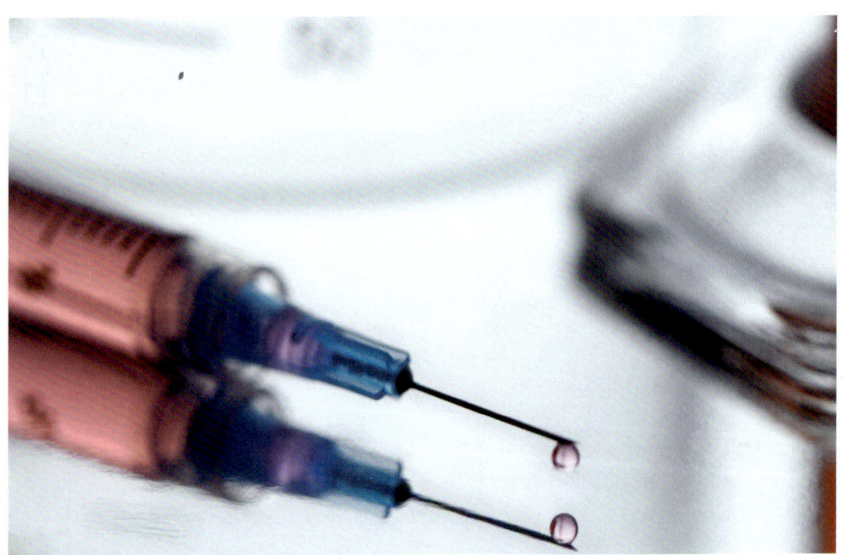

Some vaccines are swallowed; others are injected.

20   PUBLIC HEALTH

DISEASES

Recommended Childhood and Adolescent Immunization Schedule*

Vaccine ▼ / Age ►	Birth	1 month	2 months	4 months	6 months	12 months	15 months	18 months	24 months	4–6 years	11–12 years	13–18 years
Hepatitis B	HepB #1	Only if mother HBsAg(–)	HepB #2			HepB #3				HepB series		
Diphtheria, Tetanus, Pertussis			DTaP	DTaP	DTaP		DTaP	DTaP		DTaP	Td	Td
Haemophilus influenzae Type b			Hib	Hib	Hib	Hib						
Inactivated poliovirus			IPV	IPV		IPV				IPV		
Measles, Mumps, Rubella						MMR #1				MMR #2	MMR #2	
Varicella						Varicella				Varicella		
Pneumococcal			PCV	PCV	PCV	PCV	PCV			PCV / PPV		
Influenza	Vaccines below broken line are for selected populations								Influenza (yearly)			
Hepatitis A										Hepatitis A series		

Range of Recommended Ages | Catch-Up Immunization | Preadolescent Assessment | Targets age groups that may have missed vaccines recommended at an earlier age.

*This schedule reflects the recommended ages for routine childhood vaccines as of April 1, 2004, through December 2004, for children through age 18. For the most up-to-date information, visit the National Immunization Program Web site at http://www.cdc.gov/nip, or call the toll-free hotline at 800-232-2522. Information courtesy of the Centers for Disease Control and Prevention.

PUBLIC HEALTH 21

Early Detection

After a person has been exposed to a disease pathogen, some time may pass before symptoms appear. During this *incubation period,* the pathogen multiplies and spreads in the body. The incubation period for diseases varies from disease to disease, but in most cases, such as for the common cold, it is about a week. Some diseases, however, have long incubation periods, sometimes called a long *latent period.* Examples of diseases with long latent periods are tuberculosis and AIDS.

Many of the people who are infected with tuberculosis are not aware of their infection. Tuberculosis saps a person's strength and vitality. Sometimes the disease attacks the organs. It is spread by lung discharges, like coughs. AIDS is a disease that is spread through various bodily fluids, such as blood or semen. People who do not know that they have the virus that causes AIDS can spread the deadly disease for years before they show symptoms themselves.

Clearly, it is important to detect diseases as soon as possible after they develop. Public health providers can be a great help in the early detection of diseases through testing and routine screening.

> Early detection and treatment of disease greatly increase the chances of a disease being cured or its negative effects being slowed, and greatly decrease the chance that the disease is passed on to other people.

Screening Tests

Public health workers often conduct *screening tests* to discover diseases and infections among large groups of people. Screening tests usually are given in convenient, public locations such as schools, shopping centers, neighborhood health centers, or specially equipped trailers that can easily be moved and set up.

Health screening tests vary. Skin tests are used to detect allergies or tuberculosis. The test for tuberculosis is required for all commercial food preparers and handlers and for those in many other service professions. Chest *radiographs* (X-rays) are

DISEASES

used to screen for cancer, tuberculosis, and other lung diseases. Blood tests can detect AIDS, other sexually transmitted diseases, hepatitis, thyroid problems, and diabetes.

Screening tests are not meant to make a final diagnosis or to identify a disease. People who have positive results on screening tests should have more precise tests done.

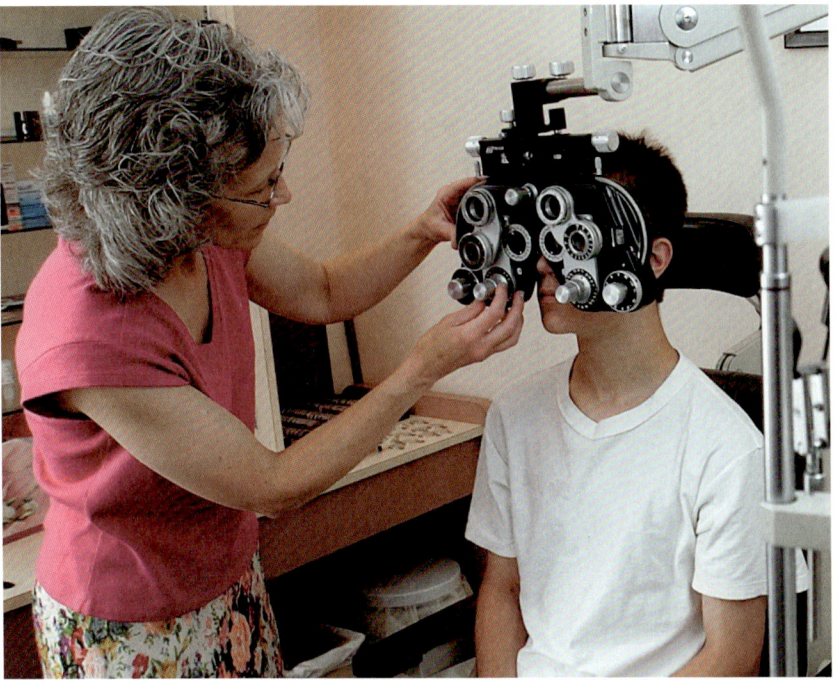

An eye screening test may show the need for glasses, detect glaucoma, or reveal color blindness.

DISEASES

Common Diseases

Hundreds of diseases around the world can infect humans. While some of these diseases might be considered "exotic" or "foreign" to the rest of the world, they could be classified as "common" diseases to the affected area and its population. Many factors help determine the spread or containment of these diseases. For instance, some diseases

- Are common and deadly in one area and not another, such as malaria and cholera
- May have been common in some parts of the world and then may start appearing in another part, such as West Nile virus in the United States
- Were once common but are now controlled, such as smallpox
- May have a limited effect because of natural barriers (forests, jungles, mountain ranges) or climate factors (such as tropical rainforest diseases)
- Are found in specific genetic populations or because of cultural practices

A *vector* is any animal or insect that can transmit a disease to a human. Flies, mosquitoes, ticks, and rats are common vectors. Covering trash, disposing of pet feces, removing standing water, and clearing debris and overgrown plants from your property will help keep vectors away. In the interest of public health, communities work together to keep vector-borne diseases at a minimum. Regular garbage pickup, mosquito surveillance and treatment, and enforcement of health codes are just some of the ways cities help control vectors.

Individuals can help prevent disease by making their living spaces inhospitable to vectors such as rats.

24   PUBLIC HEALTH

DISEASES

Some diseases are easily described; others do not fall into neat categories. For example, a virus, a bacterium, or even another source can bring on meningitis. Some diseases that generally are known as sexually transmitted diseases can be spread in other ways as well. *Vectors* such as mosquitoes and ticks spread many diseases. Other diseases are the result of environmental sources, such as secondhand smoke.

All of us should learn about common diseases in our area and what we can do to help prevent them; this is where public health starts. Following are some diseases that are common concerns for public health in the United States.

> People with the flu are contagious one day before and up to seven days after they show symptoms.

Influenza

Influenza, or the flu, is caused by a virus. It affects respiration (breathing). The symptoms include fever, muscle aches, sore throat, and a dry cough. Some people also experience nausea, vomiting, and diarrhea.

The flu is extremely contagious, and sometimes flu infections can spread around the world (called a *pandemic*). A sneeze or cough can carry flu-infected droplets through the air up to 3 feet away, where they might fall on another person or an object people share. People should cover their mouths when coughing or sneezing and frequently wash their hands; this can greatly reduce the spread of the flu.

Whenever handling food and after going to the bathroom, a thorough hand washing with soap and water will help keep you—and others—healthy.

Elderly people and people whose immune systems are weak are advised to get a flu vaccine each fall. Each year, more than 3,500 Americans die from the flu and flu-related complications such as pneumonia. Flu vaccines are available, but because the flu virus has many different strains, the vaccine may not keep a person from getting some form of the flu. There are antiviral medicines that help lessen the severity of the flu.

PUBLIC HEALTH

Hepatitis

Hepatitis is a virus that attacks the liver. There are three major types, called type A, type B, and type C. In many cases of hepatitis, a person will not have any symptoms of the disease. When symptoms do appear, they can be similar to those of the flu. *Jaundice* may also occur.

> Jaundice is the yellowing of skin and eyes. It signals that the liver is not functioning properly.

Type A hepatitis is spread through contaminated fecal matter. When people do not wash their hands well after using the bathroom and then handle food, they can pass on hepatitis to unsuspecting diners. Water can be infected by animal or human fecal matter, too. There usually is no long-term infection for hepatitis A, but types B and C can lead to serious liver disease and liver cancer.

Hepatitis B and C are spread through infected bodily fluids such as saliva, semen, and blood. An estimated 1.25 million Americans have hepatitis B, and as many as 4 million Americans have been infected with hepatitis C. Most of these people do not know they have hepatitis. There is no cure for either of these serious diseases, and the current treatments help only from 20 to 40 percent of infected people. However, a vaccine for all age groups is available for hepatitis B.

Hepatitis can be prevented by practicing good sanitation and personal hygiene, treating water that is not potable, sterilizing medical supplies and equipment, and isolating people who have hepatitis A. To prevent the spread of hepatitis, do not share razors, toothbrushes, or any other items that could have tiny amounts of blood on them. Also, when visiting countries where type E hepatitis has been found (it does not occur in the United States), drink only water that has been boiled.

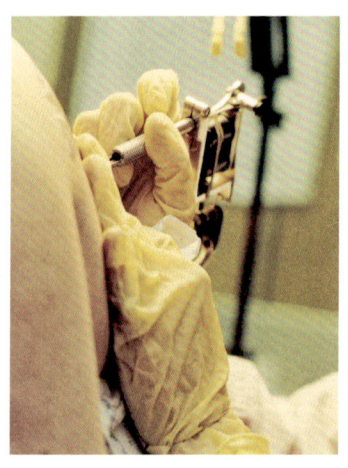

The tools of tattoo artists can transmit hepatitis.

Meningitis

Meningitis is an infection that causes inflammation of the *meninges,* the tissue surrounding the brain and spinal cord. It can be caused by many different viruses, bacteria, and even fungi.

The signs of meningitis usually include headache, high fever, and a stiff neck. There may also be sensitivity to light, vomiting, confusion or drowsiness, and a rash. The symptoms in babies include fever, refusal to eat, and difficulty in being awakened.

Viral meningitis is serious but not usually fatal. Bacterial meningitis, however, can cause brain damage, hearing loss, and death within just a few hours. That is why it is important to go to the doctor or hospital immediately if you think you have meningitis. Bacterial meningitis is treated with antibiotics. Viral meningitis may be treated with antiviral drugs or left to resolve itself. Fungal meningitis can be treated with an antifungal medicine.

Many types of meningitis are spread by respiratory and throat secretions, such as mucus and saliva. A cough can spread the bacteria or virus into the air or onto things like telephones. Wash your hands often to help avoid transferring the bacteria to yourself.

> Sometimes, small epidemics of meningitis occur among people living in close quarters—places like college dorms, day-care centers, and military barracks.

A procedure called a *spinal tap,* during which a doctor takes a sample of fluid from near the spine, lets the doctor know what kind of meningitis, if any, a person has.

Diseases

A *chronic* disease or condition is one that lasts a long time or recurs over and over. An *acute* disease or condition lasts only a short time.

Emphysema

Emphysema is a lung condition that makes it hard for a person to get enough oxygen. The small air sacs, or *alveoli*, in the lungs lose their elasticity and become much less efficient at delivering oxygen to the blood and carrying carbon dioxide away from it. As a result, people with emphysema have trouble taking deep breaths and can become very tired after walking a short distance. Emphysema can be diagnosed by examining the lungs and by testing how strongly a person can exhale.

Emphysema is a chronic condition, and it has no cure. There are many medicines that can slow down the disease's progress and reduce inflammation and possible infections. There is no immunization for emphysema.

Air pollution, airborne toxic chemicals, and heredity contribute to emphysema, but 80 to 90 percent of emphysema is caused by smoking. The best way to keep people from getting emphysema is to keep our air clean and to encourage people not to smoke. Emphysema is a serious disease that is highly preventable.

Tetanus

Tetanus is caused by a toxin formed when *Clostridium tetani* bacteria enter the body through a wound or break in the skin, most commonly through a puncture wound, such as you might get if you step on something sharp. Tetanus bacteria normally live in soil, dust, or animal droppings. Rust does not cause tetanus, but the tetanus bacteria live in *anaerobic,* or oxygen-free, conditions under rust.

The disease causes painful stiffness of muscles, *lockjaw* (the inability to open the jaw), muscle spasms, and in some cases, death. Symptoms appear from three to 21 days after infection.

Tetanus is easy to avoid because proper immunization gives complete protection. But the protection is not lifelong. Medical experts recommend a booster injection every 10 years. Most physicians will give a booster shot after any injury to a patient even if the person has been previously immunized. If the person has never received a tetanus shot, an immediate injection of tetanus antitoxin will provide protection. Tetanus immune globulin (plasma that contains antibodies) will be given to people who have tetanus, along with support or aid for respiration.

Protection against tetanus is especially important for people who spend a lot of time outdoors. Gardeners and other people who work with manure-rich soil should wear gloves for protection against tetanus.

DISEASES

Be careful when you participate in activities and hobbies that involve lead, such as soldering and stained-glass making.

Lead Poisoning

Lead poisoning is caused by breathing in or ingesting (eating or drinking) the metal lead. Lead stays in a person's body and builds up over time. Eventually, lead poisoning can harm the brain, nerves, and blood. There is no immunization against lead poisoning. Doctors can help a person get rid of some lead in his or her body, but the damage already done is permanent.

> Some people think that lead poisoning contributed to the fall of the Roman Empire because lead was commonly used in ancient times for things such as cooking utensils, water pipes, and even makeup.

If you would like to have your house or building inspected for lead, contact your local public health department.

Lead is found in many places. House paint used before 1978 may contain lead. The paint dust, flakes, and chips might be breathed in or accidentally ingested. Small children often gnaw on windowsills and other painted surfaces. They also frequently put their hands into their mouths. These practices may cause the children to ingest more lead than the adults living in the same house.

Children are especially vulnerable to lead poisoning because their growing bodies absorb lead very easily. However, children whose healthy diets include enough calcium and iron don't absorb lead as quickly as children who are not getting enough nutrients. Wash a child's hands and toys often, and use a damp sponge to keep surfaces clean of possible lead dust.

PUBLIC HEALTH

Soil can contain lead, too, from deteriorating buildings and from the lead in car exhaust. Lead pipes and solder used in older homes can add lead to the water. In older homes that have lead pipes, lead poisoning can be avoided by using cold water for drinking and making baby formula. Hot water that runs through old pipes will contain more lead than will cold water. Food or drink held in lead-glazed pottery is another source of lead buildup in a person's body.

E. Coli Poisoning

Escherichia coli is a bacterium that causes a type of food poisoning. Different strains of *E. coli* normally live in the intestines of humans and other animals and help with digestion. But some strains cause illness and others produce toxins that are among the most poisonous substances known.

There is no vaccination for *E. coli.*

The symptoms of *E. coli* poisoning can include bloody diarrhea and stomach cramps. People usually recover on their own in a week. However, serious complications can develop in children and elderly people that lead to kidney failure and death.

Eating undercooked beef or eating unwashed fruits and vegetables are ways to get an *E. coli* infection. Unpasteurized juices and alfalfa sprouts often are culprits. People with diarrhea can spread *E. coli* to others if they do not wash their hands thoroughly or if they go swimming in a public place. Be careful not to ingest water from a swimming pool, lake, or other place where even small amounts of human and animal feces may exist.

Diseases

Report any cases of food poisoning to your local health department so that public health workers can help prevent other people from getting sick by the same means you did.

Always wash your hands well after handling reptiles, amphibians, fish, and pet birds—these critters can carry salmonella bacteria.

Salmonellosis

Salmonellosis is a type of food poisoning caused by bacteria that live in the intestines of animals and are transferred by feces. Unwashed, raw vegetables are a common source of salmonella because of the dirt and fertilizer often found on them. Undercooked meats, including beef and poultry, can harbor salmonella. Unwashed eggshells and the contents of eggs can be a source of salmonella, too. The bacteria also are found on reptiles, amphibians, fish, and pet birds.

The symptoms of salmonellosis include vomiting and diarrhea, which occur 12 to 72 hours after infection. In children, the elderly, and people with weakened immune systems, salmonella poisoning can be serious and cause death. Treatment includes keeping the person *hydrated* (giving them plenty of water) and preventing the infection from spreading to others through cross-contamination by food, water, and food utensils. Most healthy people can overcome salmonellosis on their own in about a week.

> There is no vaccine for salmonellosis. The best ways to prevent illness are to eat meats that are cooked well enough to kill the bacteria; wash all fruits and vegetables; always prepare food on a clean surface using clean utensils; and avoid foods made with uncooked eggs, such as cookie dough.

DISEASES

Botulism

Botulism is caused by a nerve toxin generated by *Clostridium botulinum* bacteria. Many years ago, commercially canned foods sometimes contained botulism toxin because companies failed to heat foods enough to kill the bacterial spores. Infected cans had bulging tops and bottoms. These days, American companies rarely make such mistakes. Botulism is most often (94 percent of cases in the United States) a result of improperly home-canned foods. Oils infused with garlic or herbs and left at room temperature may also grow spores.

Symptoms appear between six hours and two weeks after a person ingests toxin-infected food. Botulism causes paralysis that moves through the body. Blurred vision, slurred speech, difficulty swallowing, and muscle weakness are signs that a person has botulism. When the paralysis reaches the breathing muscles, a person can die.

Ventilators and other supportive care in a hospital help a person stay alive while the body fights the toxin. There is no vaccine for botulism, but if diagnosed early, a patient can be treated with an antitoxin to help prevent the spread of the toxin through the blood.

Unpasteurized honey is another source of botulism poisoning. Children younger than 1 year old should never have honey because botulism in children is very serious.

AIDS

Acquired immunodeficiency syndrome is a deadly disease caused by the human immunodeficiency virus. AIDS greatly weakens a body's immune system. Many people with AIDS die of diseases that people with healthy immune systems could easily fight off.

AIDS is spread through bodily fluids such as blood and semen. Sexual contact can transmit AIDS. People who share hypodermic needles can pass blood, and AIDS, from one person to another. Babies can get AIDS from their mothers.

> There is no vaccination or cure for AIDS. There are many useful drug treatments, however, that can extend the time it takes for the HIV infection to develop into AIDS. AIDS and HIV can be diagnosed by a blood test.

Gonorrhea

Gonorrhea is a bacterial infection that most often affects the mucous membrane in the genital area. However, it can also affect the throat and anal areas. Gonorrhea, which is spread through sexual contact with an infected person, is very common. When left untreated, it can lead to serious illness.

The symptoms of gonorrhea usually are obvious in men: pain when urinating and an abnormal discharge from the penis. Symptoms in women are mild or nonexistent. However, gonorrhea can develop into a serious infection in women called *pelvic inflammatory disease.* In both men and women, untreated gonorrhea can get into the bloodstream and cause damage to organs and joints.

Once a person becomes aware of the infection, he or she must notify all those with whom there has been intimate contact. A person also can transfer gonorrhea bacteria to the eye by touching infected genitalia and then touching the eye. Gonorrhea bacteria can live for several hours outside the body, so it also is possible to get the disease from a toilet seat or a towel.

Gonorrhea is diagnosed by a urine sample or an examination of a sample of tissue or discharge. There is no vaccine, but antibiotics will clear up the infection.

DISEASES

> Sexually transmitted diseases such as gonorrhea, syphilis, herpes simplex, and AIDS can most easily and effectively be prevented by personal abstinence and following guidelines recommended by your parents or local public health agency.

Syphilis

Syphilis, a sexually transmitted disease, is caused by a corkscrew-shaped bacterium called a *spirochete*. The disease has three stages. From 10 to 90 days after the initial infection, one or more sores will appear, usually at the place where bacteria entered the body. The sores will last a few weeks, and then go away. But this doesn't mean that the disease has gone away.

In the second stage, a rash will appear, most often on the palms of the hands and soles of the feet. The rash usually doesn't itch, and a person might not notice it. During the third stage, or latent stage, the bacteria can damage organs such as the liver, eyes, and brain.

Syphilis also can affect newborn babies, who contract it from their mothers. Syphilis is very serious for babies.

Syphilis can be detected by a blood test and other laboratory tests. Syphilis can be cured with antibiotics, but the antibiotics cannot reverse the damage already done to organs in the later stages of the disease. There is no vaccine for syphilis.

If a person has any unusual sores, discharge, or rashes, he or she should see a doctor.

Herpes Simplex

Herpes simplex (types 1 and 2) is caused by a virus that lives in tissues. Type 1 usually appears on the mouth as *cold sores* or *fever blisters*. Type 2 is called *genital herpes* and appears as a cluster of tiny blisters filled with clear fluid on the genitalia or anal area. Herpes usually is passed by skin-to-skin contact with the area of the sore. Unfortunately, sores need not be present for an infected person to be contagious.

A doctor can diagnose herpes by examining the sores. There is no immunization for herpes, and no cure. Antiviral creams and pills can shorten the duration of the blisters.

> A pregnant woman with herpes must tell her doctor immediately because herpes is very serious in infants: It can cause blindness and even death. Steps can be taken to protect the baby from the herpes virus.

PUBLIC HEALTH

Diseases

Encephalitis

Encephalitis is a swelling of the brain. Many different viruses and bacteria can cause it. Well-known causes of encephalitis are the *arboviruses,* or viruses carried by ticks or mosquitoes.

Sometimes encephalitis stems from a complication of another disease. For example, syphilis is a bacterial disease that can cause swelling of the brain. Mumps, chicken pox, and streptococcus pneumonia are a few of the viral infections that can lead to encephalitis. Because so many different things can cause encephalitis, there is no vaccine and no single cure for it. Treatment depends on the type of virus or bacterium that has caused the encephalitis. For example, if the herpes virus causes the encephalitis, an antiviral herpes medicine can be used to help the infection and treat the encephalitis.

Symptoms of encephalitis range from headache and fever to unconsciousness or coma. The disease usually does not last long, but it can lead to mental impairment or disability. Untreated, encephalitis can be fatal.

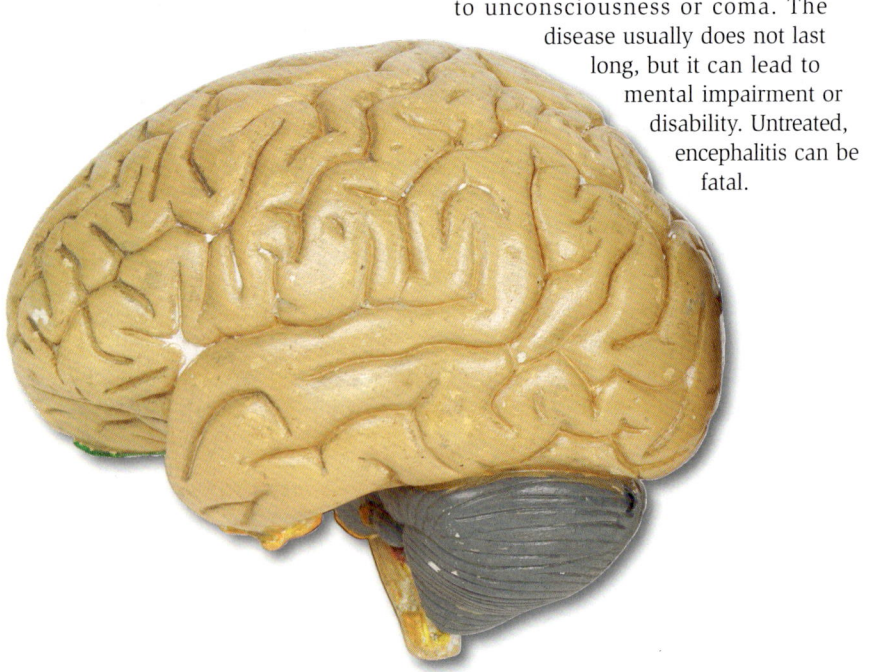

West Nile Virus

West Nile virus has been a common disease in Africa, West Asia, and the Middle East. But since about 2000, it has been occurring more and more throughout the United States and has become a concern for public health officials. WNV causes no symptoms in some people but can cause very serious problems in others. Approximately one person out of 150 who has WNV will become very ill. The victim may experience unusually severe headaches, confusion, muscle weakness, and paralysis.

Most of the time, WNV is spread by the bite of an infected mosquito. The mosquitoes become infected with the virus when they feed on infected birds or animals before biting humans. WNV can also be spread through blood transfusions. To avoid WNV, avoid getting bitten by mosquitoes. Mosquitoes lay their eggs in standing, stagnant water, so stay away from stagnant water in places such as ditches or discarded tires. Avoid swimming pools that are not chlorinated and properly maintained. Keep mosquitoes out of your home by having intact screens on windows and doors. Wear long-sleeved shirts and pants, apply insect repellent, and try to stay inside at dusk and dawn, when mosquitoes are most active.

There is no vaccine or cure for WNV. People usually get better on their own. Those who develop serious symptoms should immediately receive medical care at a hospital.

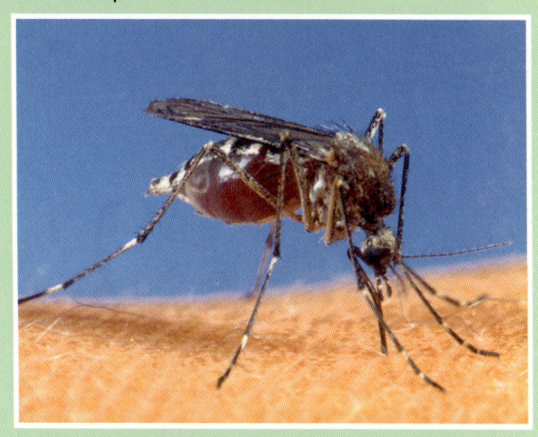

Help keep mosquitoes from breeding by eliminating stagnant water. Empty water from buckets, flowerpots, and other water traps, such as old used tires. Replace water in pet dishes and birdbaths daily.

DISEASES

Lyme Disease

Like syphilis, Lyme disease is caused by a spirochete. It is transmitted to humans by tick bites. Rodents and deer carry the bacteria in their bloodstreams. Ticks feed on those animals and then pass the disease to humans.

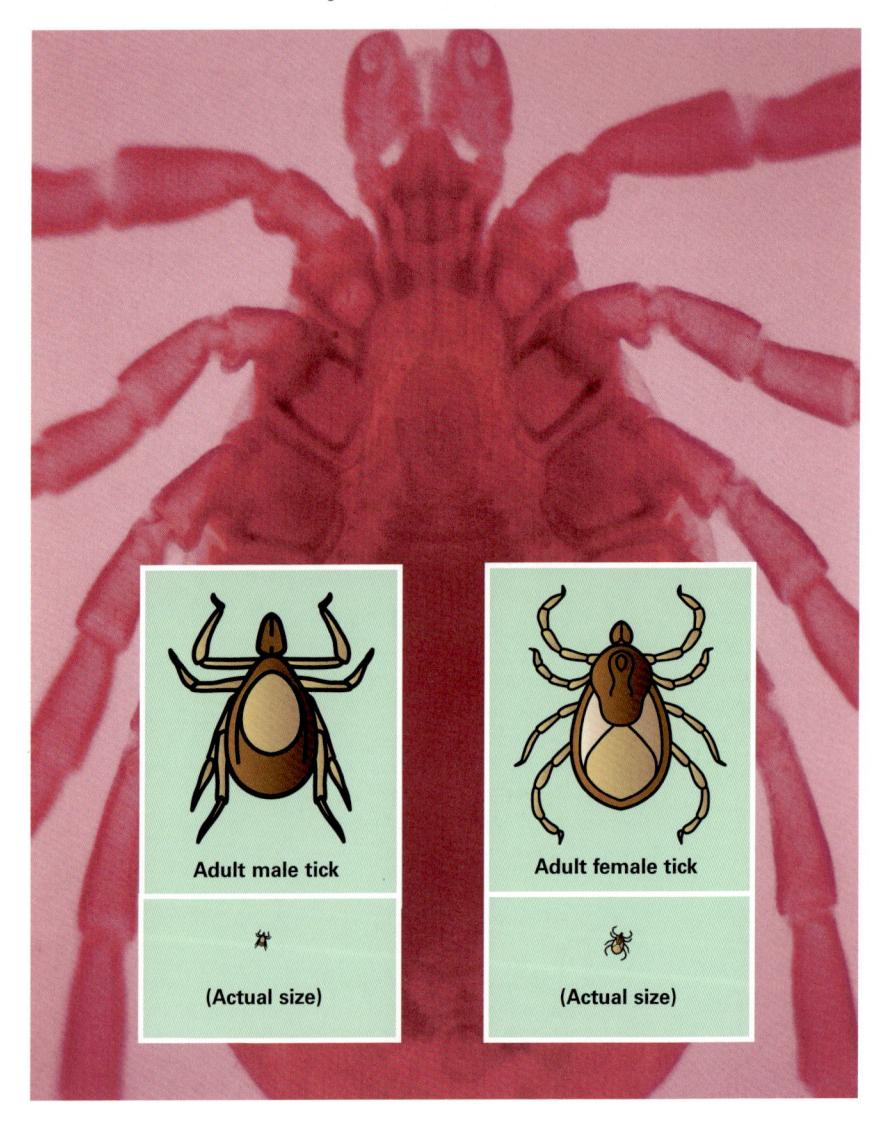

Adult male tick

(Actual size)

Adult female tick

(Actual size)

38 PUBLIC HEALTH

= Diseases

First Aid for a Tick Bite

An infected tick carries bacteria in its saliva, which it stores in its gut or salivary glands. Do not use nail polish, petroleum jelly, or a hot match to help remove a tick. Simply use tweezers or a tissue to grasp the tick as close to your skin as possible. Steadily and gently, pull up until the tick lets go. Treat the bite area of your skin with antiseptic, and contact your health-care practitioner if necessary.

Scientists think that a tick must be attached 24 hours before it can transfer the infection. Usually, a small red rash develops at the site of the bite in three to 32 days. Because the rash forms a white center, it is called a *bull's-eye rash*. Flulike symptoms may occur. Later, joint swelling, arthritis, enlargement of the heart, and other serious symptoms can develop. Lyme disease usually can be cured with a three- to four-week treatment of oral antibiotics. In more advanced cases, intravenous antibiotics may be necessary.

Lyme disease is difficult to diagnose, so keeping the tick (if you find it) is a good practice. Just put it in a container in case you need to show it to a doctor later. There is no vaccine for Lyme disease.

You can lessen your risk for Lyme disease by checking yourself for ticks when you come in from tick-infested areas. Wear long pants tucked into high socks when you walk through woods, tall grass, and underbrush. Light-colored clothing will show ticks better than dark-colored. Wear closed shoes or boots and long-sleeved shirts. Use tick or insect repellant on your clothing, but do not put it on your hands or face. Ticks are usually low, near the ground. They like shady, moist environments. Always work to keep ticks and other disease vectors away from your home.

PUBLIC HEALTH

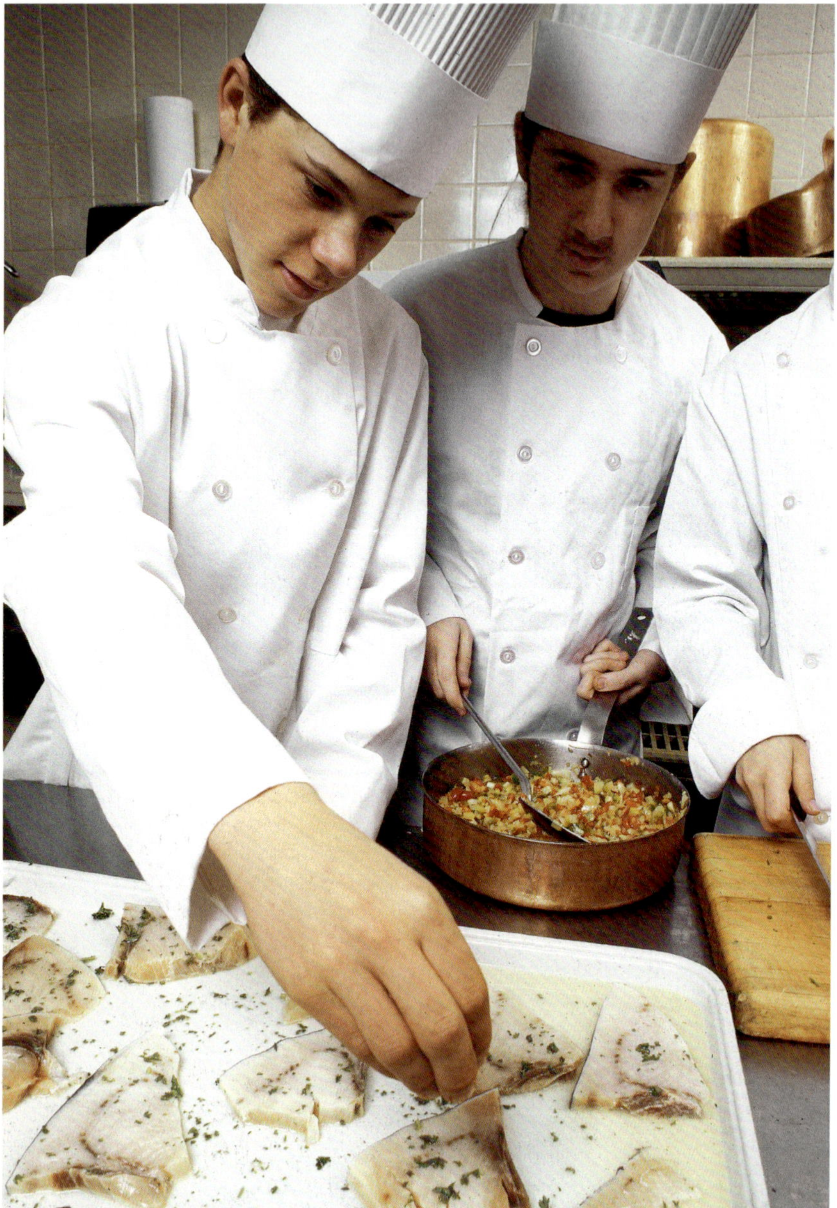

Food Sanitation

The purity of foods is an important factor in public health. Contaminated foods and drinks can spread illness. This is why public health professionals seek to improve methods of supplying food. They work to keep food free from contamination, *adulteration* (dilution or impurities), dangerous additives, and spoilage that might harm consumers.

> *Food poisoning* is caused by food that is contaminated by microorganisms such as bacteria, viruses, and parasites. *Toxic* (poisonous) substances and dangerous chemicals also can cause food poisoning. For example, some varieties of mushrooms are toxic.

The **Food and Drug Administration** is an independent agency of the U.S. government with a major responsibility for regulating food-processing plants and training inspectors and restaurant operators in safe food-handling practices. State and local health officers inspect restaurants and supermarkets to make sure they obey sanitation regulations. Some standards are voluntary. However, the fines and negative publicity that follow reports of uncleanness help to ensure that people will comply with regulations.

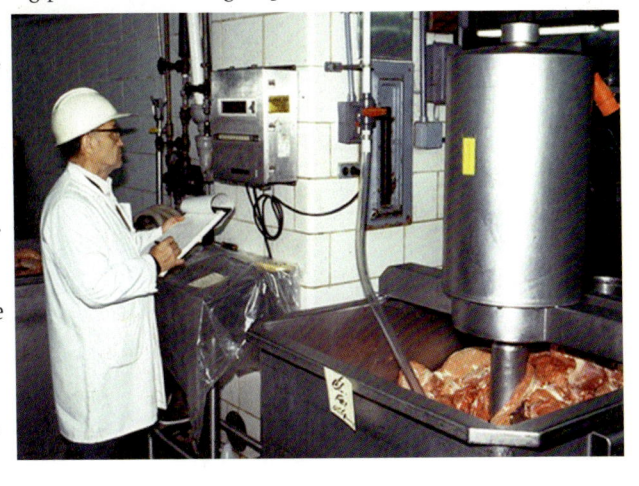

Sanitation Standards

Each year, thousands of Americans become ill from eating unsafe foods. Most cases go unreported. Many factors can cause these illnesses, but most involve carelessness by a food handler. Food should be properly processed, handled, and stored.

Food Storage

Store nonperishable foods in clean, well-ventilated, and well-lit areas on clean shelves or on pallets. Do not store food on the floor. Hold perishable foods at temperatures below 40 degrees Fahrenheit. Store frozen foods at zero degrees Fahrenheit. It is important to keep hot foods hot before serving, cold during storage, and in a vacuum (cans and vacuum jars) if storage must be at room temperature.

Do not allow foods to stay at temperatures between 40 degrees and 140 degrees for more than two hours. This temperature danger zone allows microorganisms to greatly multiply. Food that is lightly contaminated with microorganisms can be

Refrigeration does not kill microorganisms, but it keeps them from multiplying.

safe to eat, but let those microorganisms grow for more than a few hours, and you have something that can make you very sick. This is one reason to be very careful when defrosting foods.

> A good rule of thumb is to keep cold foods cold and hot foods hot. Do not defrost foods at room temperature. Instead, use the defrost setting on a microwave or defrost in the refrigerator.

Food Handling and Preparation

Even the best handling cannot improve poor-quality or unwholesome foods. People should not eat dirty or spoiled foods.

Preventing food contamination is the most reliable way to avoid food poisoning. Use screens or other coverings to protect food from contamination by insects or rodents. Keep poisons used to kill pests away from food. Keep domestic animals and pets away from food to prevent them from spreading droplets from their coughs or sneezes onto food. These discharges often contain organisms that can cause disease.

Anyone handling food must be strict about personal cleanliness, which starts with clean hands. Food preparers must wash their hands before handling any food; after using the toilet, changing a diaper, and handling pets; and after being contaminated with a cough or sneeze. Wash hands with warm water and soap; use a scrub brush if possible. Dry hands with a clean towel.

People preparing food should wear clean clothing. Street clothes may be contaminated and should be changed. Contain hair on the head with a cap, net, or a band, and contain beards with a net. Hold utensils only by their handles. Also, those who prepare food should never have any open sores on their hands.

Wash fruits and vegetables well, especially if you will be eating them uncooked. They may have been exposed to water or soil contaminated with animal or human feces, or they may have been sprayed with herbicides and pesticides.

Food preparation guidelines are as important for Scouts while camping as they are for food handlers in restaurants.

Food Sanitation

Be sure the water used in washing and preparing food and cleaning utensils and dishes is safe and comes from an approved source. Properly and safely dispose of all waste products. Proper disposal will eliminate places where flies and rodents can breed.

Food thermometers help a cook know when food has been heated enough to kill microorganisms. Food thermometers can be stuck into food such as a roast, or into a pot of boiling fruit to be made into jam.

Here are a few temperature guidelines for safe cooking:

- Ground beef, which has many small surfaces on which bacteria can grow, should be heated to at least 160 degrees.
- Roasts and steaks should be cooked to 145 degrees.
- Chicken should have an internal temperature of 180 degrees, and its juices should be clear.
- Eggs should never be eaten raw or partially cooked, including eggs used in recipes (for instance, cookie dough).

CLEANING DISHES AND UTENSILS AT HOME

Even if you use an automatic dishwasher in your home, it's important to know how to properly clean dishes by hand.

- Scrape leftover food into the trash.
- Fill the sink with hot, soapy water.
- Let dishes soak a few minutes while the water cools a bit. (Wash knives separately to avoid reaching into the suds and accidentally cutting yourself.)
- Use a clean sponge or dishrag to scrub the dishes in hot soapy water, then rinse the dishes with clean, hot water.
- Let the dishes air-dry on a rack, or use a clean cloth to dry them.

Avoid Cross-Contamination

Raw meats can contain *E. coli* and *salmonella* bacteria. That is why it is important to cook meats well before you eat them. But you must also be careful with knives, cutting boards, and other surfaces that can carry the juices of raw meat to other things. If you cut raw chicken on a cutting board and don't wash the board before using it to cut carrots, the carrots might pick up bacteria that will make you sick. An unwashed knife could spread infection the same way. Raw-meat juices also could drip from a higher shelf to a lower shelf in the refrigerator, infecting a sandwich or piece of fruit. Being aware of the dangers of cross-contamination will help you avoid small mistakes that can lead to big stomachaches.

Make ice cubes using only clean water that comes from an approved, safe water source.

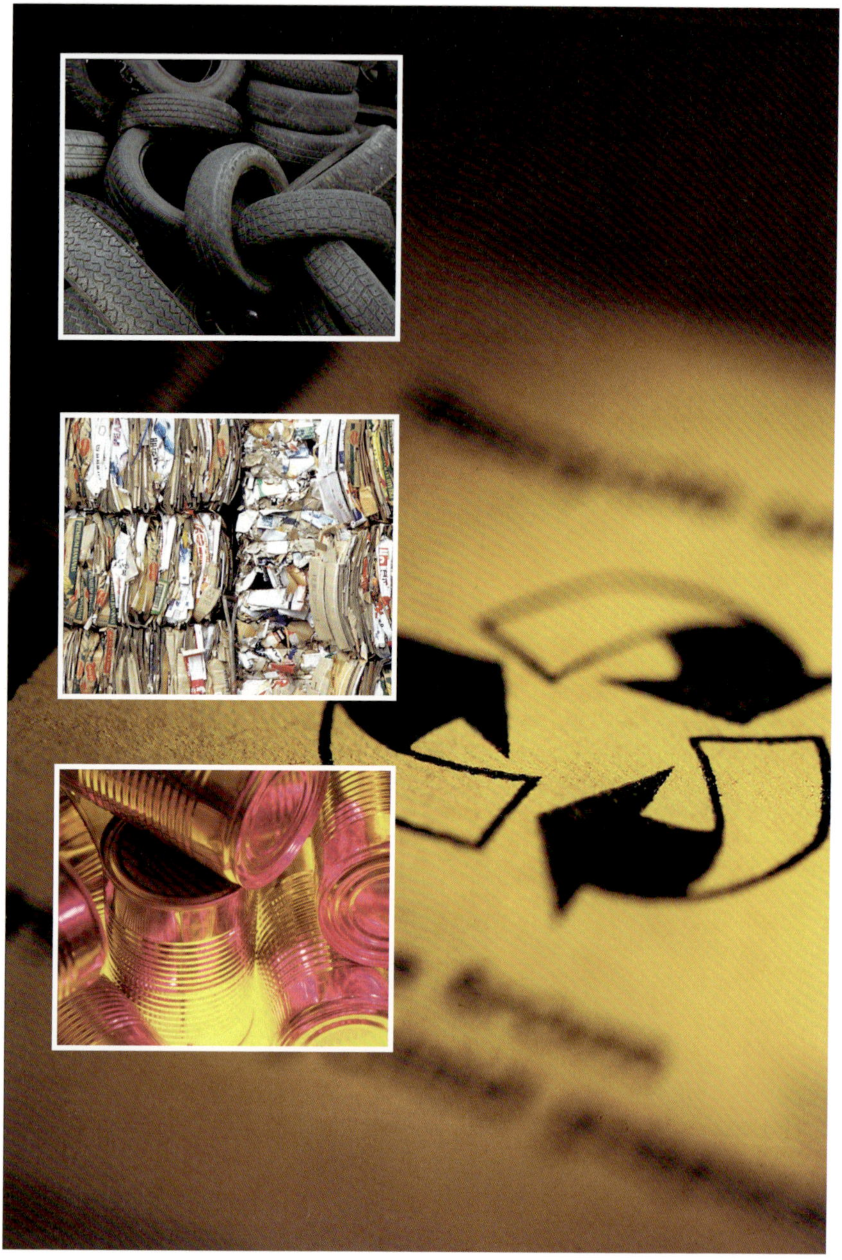

Sanitation in the Community and at Camp

Just as you work to keep your home clean for your family, public health officials work to keep your community—the public buildings, water supply, and sewage systems—working at safe levels for the entire population. At camp, there are safeguards to help ensure everyone has a healthy and safe outdoor experience.

Solid Waste Disposal

Solid waste disposal is becoming one of our society's major problems. Solid waste includes paper, cardboard, cans, bottles, plastics, food scraps, floor sweepings, industrial waste, and yard clippings. Commonly called *garbage,* solid waste often is divided into *putrescible* and *nonputrescible* waste. Items that will decompose, such as food scraps and edibles from the kitchen, are putrescible. Some putrescible items—such as yard clippings, leaves, and floor sweepings—will decompose if given enough time or if cut into small pieces. Nonputrescible items—like plastics, metals, glass, many types of paper, and construction debris—will remain virtually unchanged in a landfill. Many nonputrescible items can be recycled.

As the amount of solid waste increases each year, so does the problem of solid waste disposal. It is important to properly store and dispose of solid wastes because improper or unsanitary conditions provide breeding places for insects and rodents that can carry disease. Other problems also can exist at waste disposal sites, including fire dangers, safety hazards, and an unattractive appearance. Improper handling can sometimes lead to air and water pollution.

Sanitation in the Community and at Camp

Remember that camps and homes, as well as communities, have waste storage or disposal sites. Most insects and rodents can be controlled if storage and disposal areas are kept clean and neat. The municipal government is responsible for community waste storage and disposal. All other responsibilities for cleanliness belong to homeowners and individuals.

Wastes usually are collected and disposed of under the direction of a municipal authority. Public workers or private contractors may do this work. Most waste goes to a landfill to be buried. In urban areas, the landfill might be far from the city that creates the waste. There are accepted methods for creating and operating landfills.

> One difference between a landfill and a dump is that a landfill is covered with dirt at the end of each day.

Some wastes are burned, or *incinerated*. Compared with landfills, incinerators have both advantages and disadvantages. Burning reduces the amount of wastes, and the heat from incinerator facilities is often used to generate power. However, removing toxic wastes, ensuring that all waste is completely burned, and keeping harmful substances from entering the air are technically difficult. Ash from incinerators must be buried.

Recycling

Incinerators can create air pollution. Landfills take a lot of space, and no one wants to live near a landfill. One way to reduce the need for new waste disposal facilities and to make existing landfills more efficient is to recycle.

A number of items that go into landfills and incinerators can be recycled. Many plastics, metals, building materials, yard clippings, leaf litter, and paper can be recycled. Recycling helps to conserve natural resources because it reduces the amount of solid waste being sent for disposal. The more material that is removed from the *waste stream* (the total volume of solid wastes produced), the longer existing landfills can operate.

Sanitation in the Community and at Camp

In communities that aggressively recycle, the volume of waste material has been reduced by up to 25 percent. Unfortunately, communities with aggressive recycling programs are in the minority.

Waste Storage and Disposal at Home and at Camp

At home and in camp,

- Use approved containers to hold solid wastes until they can be collected or disposed of properly.
- Make storage facilities convenient and sanitary.
- Use containers that are strong, rust resistant, watertight with tight-fitting lids, and easily filled, emptied, and cleaned.
- Keep containers clean.

You can help your storage situation at home by using racks or stands outside that will keep containers about 18 inches above the ground and allow easy cleaning. Storage racks are easily made from wood, pipe, or metal. Concrete pads on the ground are acceptable, but raised racks are preferable.

Waste disposal in camp is often more difficult than at home. Camps, however, are bound by the same regulations as any business in the community. Waste must be disposed of correctly while at camp or on the trail. Camps should have enough approved containers (cans or bins) to hold all wastes that normally are generated between collections.

At camp, store filled plastic bags inside metal containers for better cleanliness and to make it harder for animals to gain access.

PUBLIC HEALTH

Sanitation in the Community and at Camp

> When camping in the wilderness, set a goal to leave no trace that humans were ever there. Always pack out everything that was packed in, including all wrappers, cans, boxes, foil, and food scraps. Pack recyclable items separately to be disposed of properly after the trip.

Burning solid waste on the trail creates both a fire hazard and odors that can attract animals. It also will likely conflict with the land manager's policy. Food scraps can draw animals close to campsites where they might lose their fear of humans. That can be dangerous for them and for you. Animals can detect and dig up buried trash, which also creates potential sites where mosquitoes can breed.

Latrines and Catholes

Human bodily waste can be buried if sanitary facilities are not available. If you will be camping in the same area for a few days, you will want to build a latrine. Otherwise, on the trail, digging catholes for disposal of bodily wastes is recommended because flies and rodents breed in human and animal waste. Using a stick, small trowel, or the heel of a boot, dig a hole 6 to 8 inches deep. (You will want several inches of soil to cover the hole later.) Locate catholes at least 200 feet from any body of water, the trail, and the campsite. When you are done, cover the hole completely with loose soil, tamping down lightly. Leave the site in a natural condition.

Water and Wastewater Treatment

Unsuitable water can cause infection and disease. Some water can contain contaminants like lead, mercury, and pesticides. It can also harbor microorganisms that cause diseases such as cholera, salmonellosis, and hepatitis. Drinking water must be treated and monitored. Water in recreational facilities such as water parks, swimming pools, and lakes should not be swallowed or placed in your mouth. Trace amounts of animal and human feces can infect water, as can naturally occurring bacteria and parasites.

> There are many microscopic parasites in water that are difficult to kill. Among them, *Cryptosporidium parvum* is a microscopic parasite that is difficult to kill because of its hard outer shell. Chlorine does not always do the job. Avoid swallowing water when you swim, even in a chlorinated pool. The disease *Cryptosporidiosis* causes diarrhea and fever and is the reason that drinking water should be prepared by both filtering and chemical treatment or by boiling. Both the disease and the parasite are called "Crypto" for short.

Safe Water

Water from all city water supplies must be tested regularly. Federal and state governments have created strict standards that must be maintained for *pH* (acidity), color, *particulates* (small particles), taste, and chemicals.

Some communities draw their water from deep underground *aquifers* (groundwater). In many parts of the country, drinking water is drawn from surface sources rather than underground aquifers. Water must be treated, usually by screening, filtration, and chemical applications. Municipal water is stored in tanks—generally above the ground so that gravity will provide water pressure—and delivered to homes by a network of distribution pipes.

Treating Drinking Water at Camp

Finding safe water when camping might be tough. Most modern campgrounds and park facilities have safe water available. But surface water—even water that looks clear and inviting—might not be safe to drink.

The safest attitude is to assume that all water from an aboveground source—such as a lake, stream, river, pond, or creek—must be treated. Many *subsurface* (groundwater) sources of water, such as wells, are polluted, and that water must be treated before it can be considered safe to consume. Polluted water can be successfully treated in the field, unless contaminated by chemical pollutants. (Most chemical pollutants are of human origin, but a few occur naturally.)

If you need to filter water containing silt or organic contaminants before disinfecting it, collect the water in a container and let the particles settle to the bottom of the container. Drive four stakes into the ground and tie the corner of a clean cloth to each stake. Gently pour the water through the top of the cloth and let it filter through into a second container below.

Boiling, Filters, and Chemical Treatment

Bringing water to a rolling boil for a full minute or more will kill most organisms. Boiling is the best way to treat your own water. When you are at elevations higher than 6,500 feet, boil the water for three minutes to be sure all organisms are killed.

You also can use a combination of filters and chemical treatment tablets to treat your water.

FILTERS

Camping stores and catalogs offer water treatment filters that are easy to use. Follow the instructions that come with the filter you have. According to the CDC, filters that stop Crypto and *Giardia lamblia* (a tiny parasite) will have one of these four claims on the package:

- Reverse osmosis
- *Absolute* pore size of 1 micron or smaller
- Tested and certified by NSF Standard 53 or NSF Standard 58 for cyst *removal*
- Tested and certified by NSF Standard 53 or NSF Standard 58 for cyst *reduction*

Bringing water that has been filtered to a full rolling boil for a minute or longer is the best option for treating water.

Crypto may *not* be filtered out by filters that say the following:

- *Nominal* pore size of less than 1 micron
- One micron filter
- Effective against parasites
- Carbon filter
- Water purifier
- EPA approved*
- Activated carbon

---

*Warning: The EPA does **not** approve or test filters.

Sanitation in the Community and at Camp

Most filters that you can carry on a campout don't filter out viruses. Also, even well-made filters might have flaws that allow some organisms to pass through accidentally. That is why it is important to use chemical treatment tablets on the water as well.

Because the straining cartridges on filters have collected organisms from the water, the person who changes the cartridge should be in good health and wear gloves while changing the cartridge. That person should dispose of the filter properly, and then wash his or her hands.

TABLETS

Water treatment tablets are sold in small containers just the right size for hikers and campers. The instructions on the label usually are to drop one or two tablets into a quart of water and then wait 30 minutes before drinking—longer if the water is cold. The tablets might also leave a chemical taste in the water. To improve the flavor, add some flavored drink mix *after* the tablets have had enough time to do their work.

Chemical treatment tablets kill many—but not all—bacteria, viruses, and parasites. *Cryptosporidium parvum, Giardia lamblia,* and some bacteria will not be killed. That is why the tablets alone don't guarantee safe drinking water.

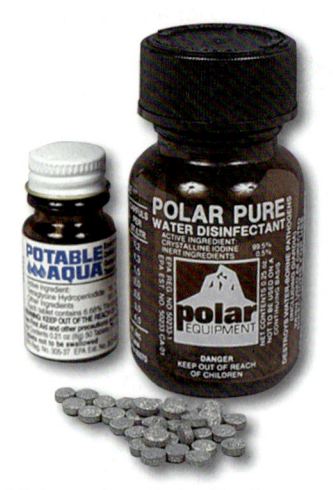

Treatment tablets can lose their effectiveness after the bottle has been opened. Check the expiration date on the label and use only fresh tablets.

Dishwashing in Camp

Whether you cook with a stove or over an open fire, put on two pots of water before you serve a meal. That way you will have hot dishwater by the time you finish eating.

Set up the dishwater. Boil a pot of water. Add a small amount of biodegradable dishwashing liquid and some cold treated water so that you can use it without burning your hands.

Set up the rinse water. In a second large pot, boil water to rinse the dishes.

Wash the dishes. Scrape all excess food on the plate into a garbage or plastic bag that you will pack out. Then (a) scrub the dish in the wash water and (b) use tongs to rinse the clean dish in hot rinse water, or (c) if you want to use a cold rinse, dip dishes in cold water that has been treated. Allow dishes to air-dry on a clean, plastic sheet. When dry, store in a flyproof container.

Dispose of the dishwater. When you are finished washing dishes, strain food particles from the dishwater. Put the food particles in a resealable plastic bag that you will pack out. Then take the water at least 200 feet from the campsite, water source, and trails. Give it a good fling, spreading it over a wide area.

Sanitation in the Community and at Camp

Never put anything into a water source that you would not be willing to drink.

You can make a strainer by punching small holes in a plastic bag and filling it with pine needles. Pour dirty dishwater through the bag and the needles will strain out food particles. Carry the bag of needles out of the backcountry with the rest of your trash.

Keep Soap and Detergent Away From Open Water

Many soaps, detergents, and shampoos contain chemicals that encourage algae to grow. Algae can crowd out native plants, making it harder for fish and other animals to survive. Soap and detergent can leave an oily film in water that can harm tiny aquatic life. Even biodegradable soap should be kept away from any stream, lake, or spring. Carry your pot of water away from the source, and use it to bathe or wash dishes. Scatter water over the ground, across a wide area, when you are finished.

Sewage and Liquid Waste

Sewage has the potential to spread disease, so it must be properly disposed of both at home and at camp. Wastewater from toilets is called *blackwater.* Water from washing dishes, bathing, and doing laundry is called *graywater.* If discharged improperly, either type of wastewater can contribute to water pollution.

Most urban and suburban dwellers in the United States dispose of sewage and liquid wastes through municipal disposal systems. In rural areas of the country, many homeowners have their own septic systems for household waste.

= SANITATION IN THE COMMUNITY AND AT CAMP

Requirement 5a calls for a visit to a municipal wastewater treatment facility like this one, or to a solid-waste management operation in your community.

Municipal Sewage Treatment Systems

Municipal sewage treatment systems are designed to handle large volumes of sewage and liquid wastes. The raw sewage flows to a treatment plant through underground pipes *(mains)*. Sewage is screened, allowed to settle, processed, dried, and disinfected before disposal.

Screening removes objects larger than an inch or two in size that have entered sewage mains. The screens are periodically cleaned. Debris is removed and then taken to a landfill or burned.

By the time incoming waste reaches the sewage treatment plant, it is mostly liquid with particles suspended in it. Many suspended particles drop out of the liquid portion as the screened sewage is allowed to settle.

Processing or treatment is done by two basic methods: *activated sludge* and *trickling.* In both methods, bacteria break down the sewage into harmless components that can be safely discharged.

In the activated sludge method, the sewage is pumped into a tank. Air is bubbled through the sewage to provide oxygen needed by the bacteria. After the bacteria have worked on the sewage long enough, the liquid contents of the tank can be pumped out. The material remaining at the bottom of the tank, called sludge, can be dried.

PUBLIC HEALTH   57

Sanitation in the Community and at Camp

Apartment complexes, shopping centers, camps, and similar properties will sometimes have a small sewage treatment plant on their grounds. This type of plant operates on the same principles as an activated sludge plant, only on a smaller scale.

Trickling involves filtering the sewage over a bed of rocks on which bacteria grow. In time, the liquid can be pumped out and the accumulated sludge dried. The sludge, after drying, can be buried in a landfill or used as a soil conditioner.

Treated wastewater is usually clear. At this point, the water is free of contaminants and can be pumped into a river or other body of water for disposal. In some states, the water is piped to automatic lawn sprinklers and used to recharge underground water supplies. The outflow from modern treatment plants is so high in quality that it can go to a chlorinating station and be reused for drinking water.

Septic Systems

Millions of homes have their own septic systems. Homes that are built far from municipal mains, such as homes in rural areas, use septic tanks.

Wastewater from the home flows through a pipe into the septic tank, which is made of material such as concrete or steel. Solids settle to the bottom of the tank, and liquid flows out into a series of buried pipes. The liquid trickles through holes in the pipes and enters the gravel and soil of the *leach field.* The water seeps through the field and is cleaned of organic material—not with harsh chemicals, but with microorganisms that live in the soil. Eventually, this water will enter an underground aquifer (a naturally occurring water basin).

= SANITATION IN THE COMMUNITY AND AT CAMP

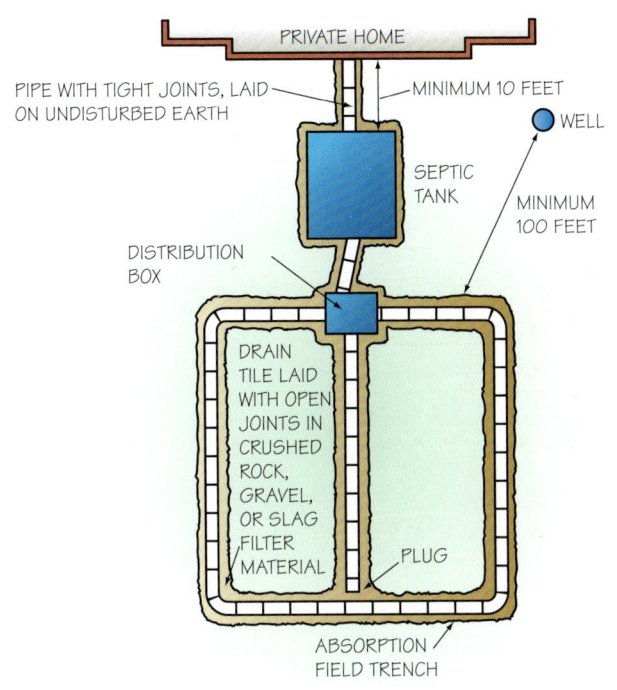

A home septic system

Bacteria break down some of the solids that remain behind in the tank. That is why chemicals that can kill bacteria should not be put into the septic system. Medicines such as antibiotics will destroy helpful bacteria. Motor oils, gasoline, paints, solvents, pesticides, and herbicides will do the same thing. Grease, paper towels, and excessive amounts of food will not kill bacteria but will clog the pipes.

The sludge in the septic tank should be pumped out by a professional every two to five years, depending on the size of the tank and the number of people using it.

Leach fields should be at least 100 feet from any drinking water supply. The fields should be checked every year to make sure they are not flooding.

PUBLIC HEALTH 59

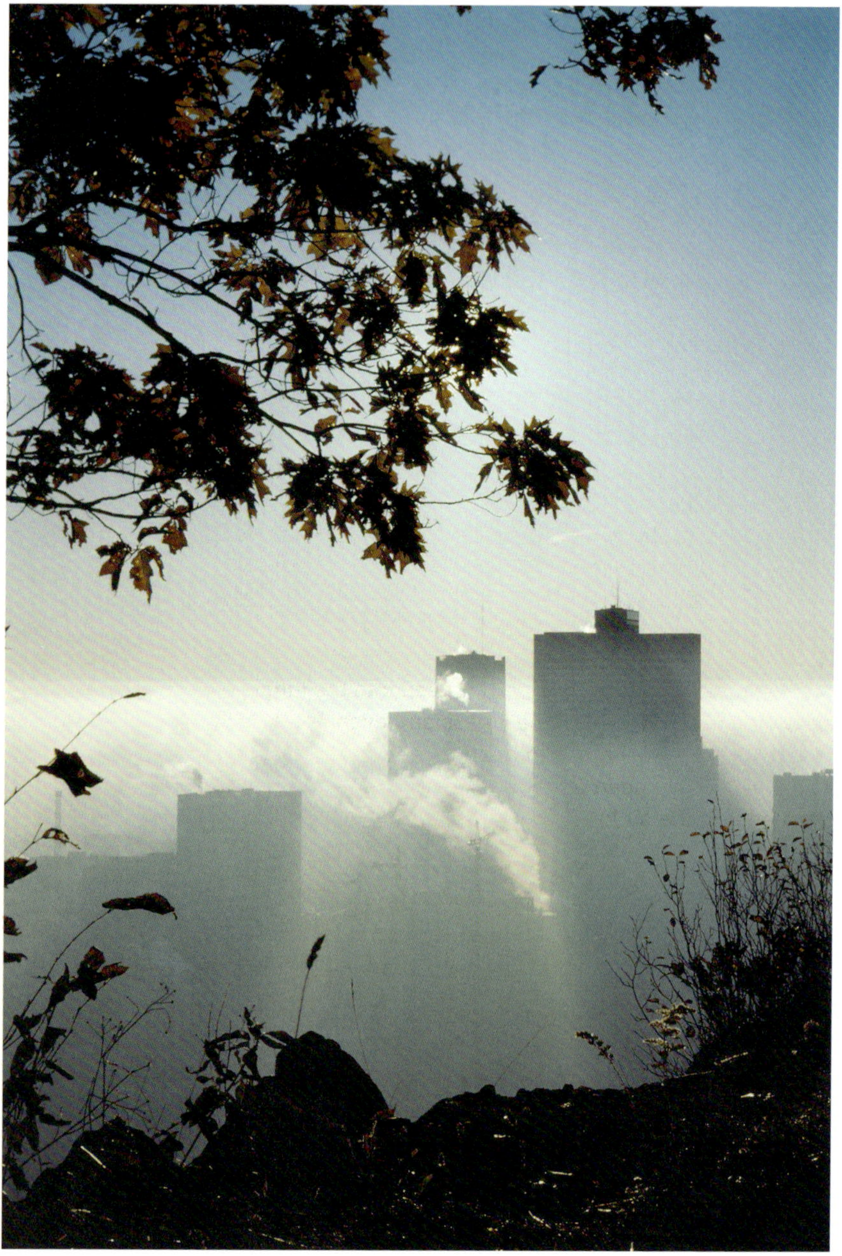

Pollution and Health

Environmental pollution—including air, water, and noise pollution—affects individual and public health in many serious ways. Pollutants can enter the body as a person breathes, eats, or drinks, and through the eyes, nose, ears, and skin.

Air Pollution

The major sources of air pollution are automobiles, power plants, and factories. They burn fuels, including fossil fuels such as natural gas, oil, or coal, that send unhealthy chemicals and particulates into the air. Dry-cleaning chemicals, wildfires, and decomposing garbage, which gives off methane gas, are a few of the many other sources of air pollution.

> *Particulate matter* can easily get deep into the lungs. Inhaled particulates cause illness and even death. For instance, people with heart disease are more likely to have heart attacks when the particulate matter in the air is high.

Drops of sulfur dioxide and oxides of nitrogen can combine with moisture and turn into *acid rain*, which can pollute our water supplies and our land.

Ozone is a form of oxygen, but it can be a poison. It forms in the lower atmosphere, or *troposphere*, from nitrogen oxides and organic gases from automobiles and industry. High levels of it irritate everyone's lungs, but especially people with asthma, bronchitis, and emphysema. Ozone can also kill trees and damage rubber. Scientists are investigating the many possible effects of breathing in ozone.

The ozone layer, however, far up in the part of the atmosphere called the *stratosphere*, helps protect Earth from the damaging rays of the sun. Since the 1970s, scientists have been

PUBLIC HEALTH

concerned that the ozone layer is depleting because of our use of various chemicals that react with the ozone and destroy it. The depletion of the protective ozone layer makes everything on Earth more exposed to radiation from the sun, which increases incidences of cancer. Though we don't want ozone in our troposphere, we need it up high in our stratosphere.

The **Environmental Protection Agency** monitors and sets standards for air quality. It also regulates many sources of air pollution. As new scientific studies are published about air pollution and the public health, the EPA wants to set stricter rules to limit air pollution.

There are two basic ways to prevent air pollution. *End-of-the-pipe* devices filter some of the chemicals and particles out of exhaust from factories and automobiles. The catalytic converter used on cars is an example of this type of device.

Until we learn more about how to prevent pollution, we can at least try to control and minimize it. Manufacturing can be designed to produce less waste. Individuals can drive less—and instead take advantage of public transportation, carpooling, and bicycling. We can all become aware of how important and far-reaching issues of air pollution are.

= POLLUTION AND HEALTH

The greenhouse effect

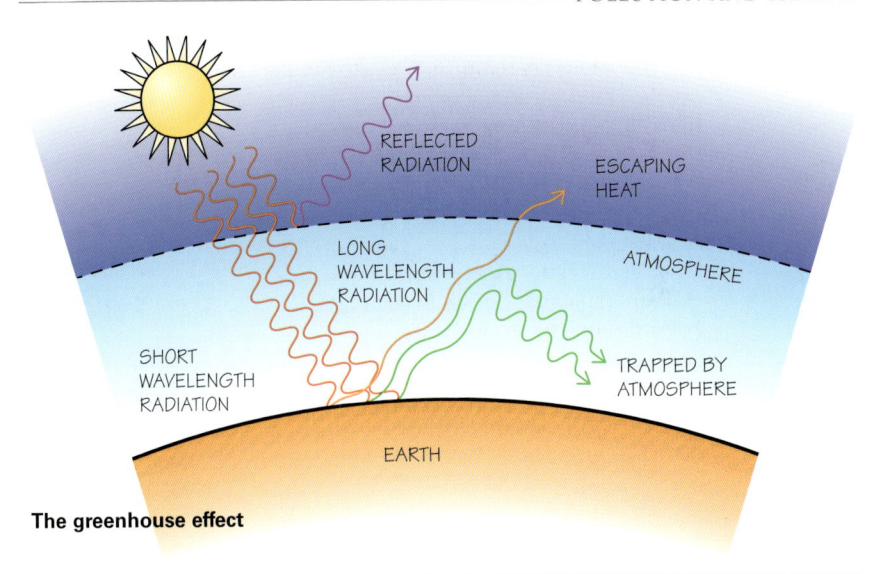

The Greenhouse Effect

Gases such as carbon dioxide and methane collect in the atmosphere. They reflect heat from the ground back on Earth, warming it. This situation may cause long-term climatic changes to our *ecosystems*. Some species of animals may have to change habitats. Although there is some scientific evidence of what is popularly called global warming, many scientists remain skeptical about it.

Water Pollution

Only about 2 percent of the world's water is available for drinking. During the 20th century, much of the world's available freshwater supply became polluted. The overall population growth and expansion of cities make maintaining water quality challenging.

There are two main sources of water pollution. *Point sources* are easy to recognize. For example, a factory dumping chemical waste directly into a river is a point source of water pollution. *Nonpoint sources* are harder to detect, track, and stop. These sources pollute the water indirectly. For example, buried waste, including landfills and buried hazardous wastes, can leach into water supplies.

> An *ecosystem* is a community of organisms and their environment, all working together as a unit.

PUBLIC HEALTH   63

POLLUTION AND HEALTH

Herbicides, pesticides, fertilizers, and other chemicals are another source of pollution. Rain can wash the chemicals and soil into nearby streams, rivers, and lakes. Also, the chemicals can soak down into the ground, where they can end up in an aquifer.

Lead, mercury, pesticides, and other toxic ingredients of polluted water can build up in our bodies and cause acute illnesses, like diarrhea, and chronic ones, like organ damage and cancer. Indirectly, polluted water can affect us by way of the food chain. If a plant uses water that is contaminated with a toxic chemical, and then we eat that plant, we can ingest that chemical. If we eat an animal that ate that plant, the concentration of the chemical is even higher.

Water pollution adversely affects all kinds of living things. Detergent can ruin an ecosystem by allowing an overgrowth of plants and algae. When those greater-than-normal amounts of plants and algae die, the decomposition depletes the oxygen in the water. Fish suffocate and die, and other wildlife higher up the food chain suffers as well.

A nonpoint source of pollution occurs when automobiles drip engine oil into the street, then rain washes that oil into the gutters, and then into streams and rivers.

= POLLUTION AND HEALTH

Watershed dams like the one shown here help control runoff from streams and hold and store polluting sediment. Wherever you live, you are in a watershed.

People can safeguard water supplies in many ways. We can protect *watersheds*—the land areas from which water drains into rivers and lakes. Controlling chemical contamination of water is a high priority. Industrial chemicals are relatively easy to control when factories follow EPA guidelines. People can be careful of what goes into storm drains and not dump used engine oil, automobile coolant, paint, and other chemicals into the street. Homeowners can limit their use of pesticides, herbicides, and fertilizers on their lawns or use organic methods of lawn care and gardening instead. Campers can avoid using detergents near streams and other groundwater sources.

If they aren't used with caution, headphones can be especially damaging to your hearing.

Noise Pollution

Unwanted or loud noises are pollutants, too. Excessive noise can lead to hearing loss, headaches, and stress. Some people live where they are regularly subjected to loud noises. Machinery, automobiles, and trucks can all be noisy. Radios, stereos, and other entertainment equipment also contribute to hearing loss. Headphones are great for sparing the people around someone who is listening to music, but they concentrate noise in the listener's ears and can damage them.

The damage caused by noise is cumulative—it adds up over time. With each exposure to loud noises, a person suffers a tiny—often unnoticeable—loss of hearing. Eventually, the hearing loss becomes significant.

> Rock musicians often wear earplugs when performing to protect their hearing. Fans who sit in front of loudspeakers may suffer *transient,* or temporary, hearing loss from a few hours to a few days after a concert.

Noise also happens at home. Power tools, lawn mowers, and televisions contribute to noise pollution. Indoor appliances such as blow-dryers and vacuum cleaners make noise. Some hobbies can be noisy, such as shooting sports and woodworking power tools. Also noisy are recreational vehicles such as motorboats, snowmobiles, motorcycles, and cars without

POLLUTION AND HEALTH

mufflers. In addition to hearing loss, noise can contribute to stress (physical and mental), sleep loss, and irritability, and can lead to health-related problems such as depression, gastrointestinal problems, and cardiovascular disease.

The technology exists to reduce noise pollution. Jet engines are much quieter now than they used to be. Buildings are being designed that limit noise. The **Occupational Safety and Health Administration** regulates noise in workplaces, requiring employers to reduce noise exposure that could be harmful to employees. However, noise-reduction programs require commitment and money. People should wear hearing protection wherever noise either is not or cannot be controlled. Most hearing loss is permanent; most of it also is preventable.

Noise pollution harms more than just humans. It has been shown that aircraft noise reduces the survival rate of caribou calves. Marine life is harmed by noise in the oceans from offshore drilling and ship traffic. Sonar—the sending of sound waves to detect military submarines and to chart the ocean floor—can be damaging to whales that use their own natural sonar to survive.

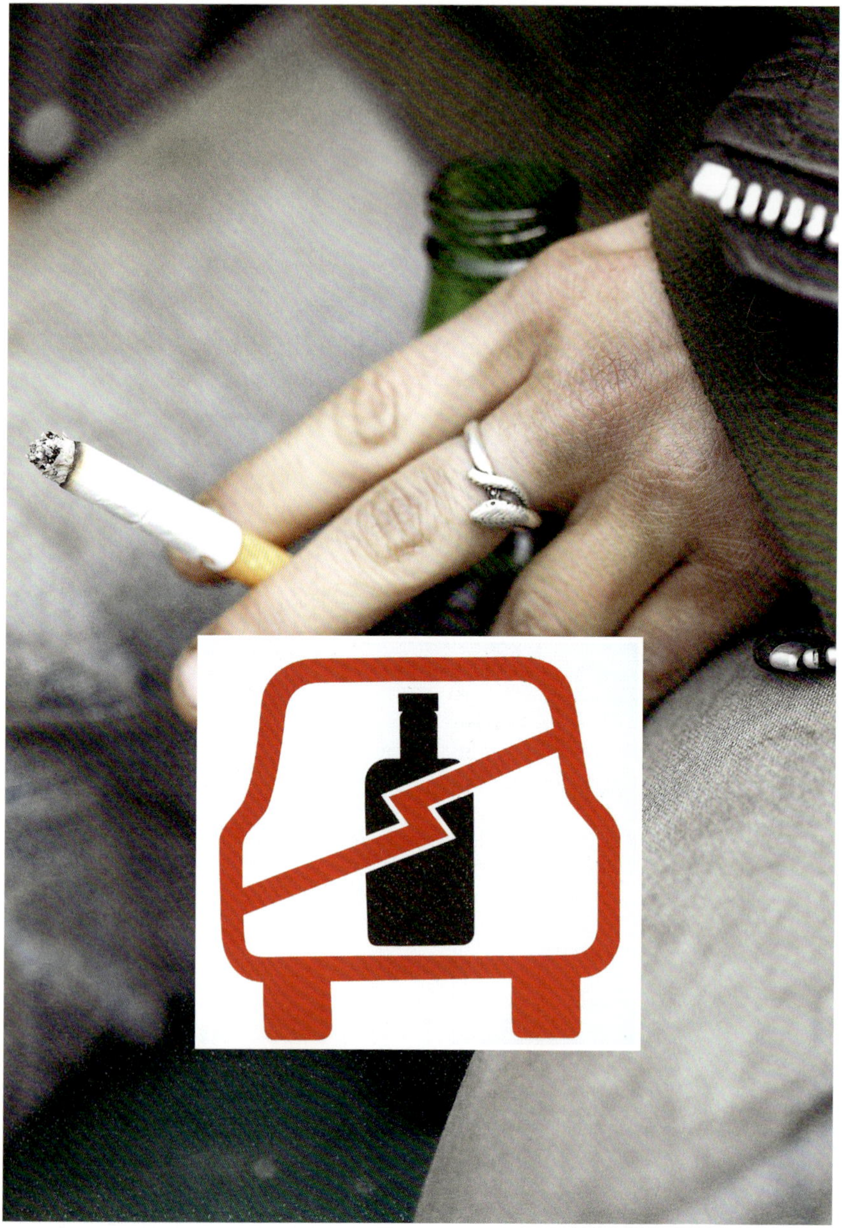

Tobacco, Alcohol, and Drugs

Tobacco, alcohol, and illegal drugs are a significant source of morbidity and mortality in the United States and around the world. The World Health Organization considers tobacco use to be an *epidemic* because it kills 4.2 million people every year. Using these substances can damage the body, lead to accompanying diseases, and cause great numbers of injuries and accidents.

Tobacco

Tobacco contains more than 4,000 chemical compounds, many of which cause emphysema and cancer. In fact, cigarette smoking causes 87 percent of lung cancer—a rarely cured disease with survival rates of no more than five years and the third-leading cause of death in the United States, behind cardiovascular disease and stroke. Smoking contributes greatly to those diseases as well.

About 80 percent of smokers began smoking before they were 18 years old. Because nicotine is one of the most addictive substances known to humans, young adults who start using tobacco often become hooked for life. Smoking also causes many diseases that affect indirect users, such as people who inhale secondhand smoke and unborn babies who suffer the effects of their mothers' addiction to tobacco.

Tobacco, Alcohol, and Drugs

Being personally responsible to yourself is part of growing up. Remember that the decisions you make go hand in hand with their consequences.

Smokeless tobacco—chewing tobacco and snuff—is dangerous, too. The *carcinogens,* or cancer-causing agents, act on the cheeks and gums at the spot where a user keeps a chaw of tobacco. The carcinogens don't stop at the mouth—tobacco use increases the incidence of all kinds of cancers.

Smoking tobacco affects the skin's chemistry, causing it to age much faster than normal, so smokers get more wrinkles at an earlier age than do nonsmokers. Tobacco contributes to tooth decay, gum disease, and early loss of teeth.

Alcohol

Alcohol can injure your body, especially your liver and brain. Alcohol is absorbed through the stomach, enters the bloodstream, and is processed by the liver. A deadly disease that can be caused by the overconsumption of alcohol is *cirrhosis* of the liver. Over time, this disease causes the liver to malfunction. Alcohol also can damage the digestive system, pancreas, and nervous system. Heavy drinkers are prone to oral and throat cancers, and liver cancer. Alcohol also can cause serious damage to unborn children.

Alcohol is a *sedative;* it interferes with reflexes and brain function. It makes people react slowly to their environment. People who are intoxicated have trouble walking, speaking, and driving. Sometimes people who drink too much alcohol die because their body becomes so *sedate,* or slow, that their breathing and heart rate simply slow to a stop.

70   PUBLIC HEALTH

Tobacco, Alcohol, and Drugs

Although you might be too young to drive a car, be aware of the dangers of drinking and driving. Even a small amount of alcohol can make a person an unsafe driver, and the results are often tragic. Thousands of teenagers die every year in crashes involving drivers who have been drinking. Never ride in a car being driven by someone who has been drinking. Never let someone who has been drinking drive a vehicle. You can always find another way home, but you might not live through a crash caused by a drunken driver.

Drugs

Drugs are chemicals that alter the body's chemistry. Young people should never use illegal drugs or drugs that don't come from their doctors. Marijuana, cocaine and crack, codeine, depressants, LSD, heroin, inhalants, and steroids have powerful effects on the mind and the body. They can produce temporary feelings of pleasure or energy. However, they also can cause nightmares, fear, and loss of reason. **An overdose can lead to serious illness, disability, or even death.**

Drug users often take risks that endanger their safety and well-being. People have drowned, fallen to their deaths, and died in motor vehicle crashes while under the influence of drugs. Besides deaths due to accidents, deaths are also attributed to the spread of the virus that causes AIDS through using commonly shared drug paraphernalia. Many drug users first acquire HIV from indiscriminate drug usage, and they may then pass the disease on sexually to others, even to people who don't use drugs.

Many drugs are addictive. Once a person uses a drug, he or she might soon have an uncontrollable desire for it. Users might lie, cheat, and steal to get the drug, or their "fix." It can be physically and emotionally painful to stop using the drug. Using drugs can become more important to them than friends, family, and even their own lives.

Be a leader and use your own good judgment. Stay away from drugs and drug users.

= Tobacco, Alcohol, and Drugs

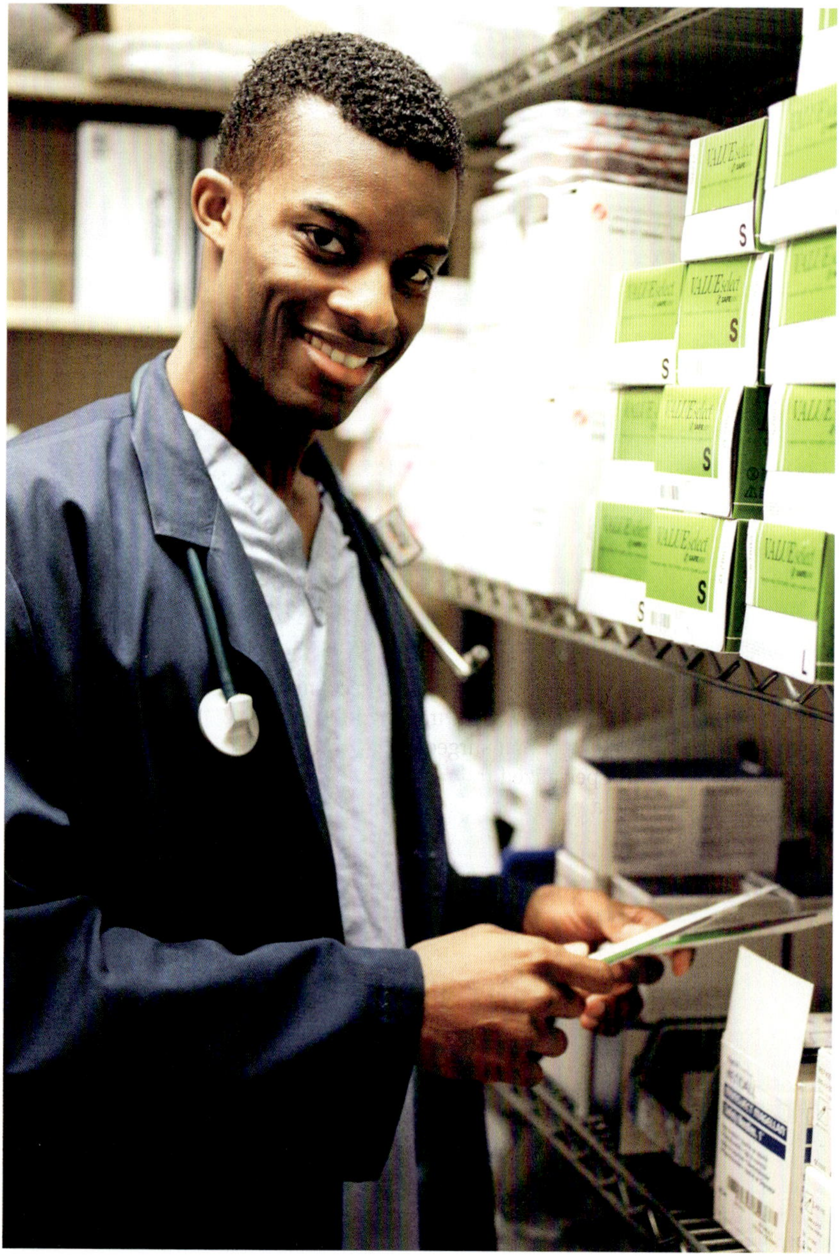
VALUEselect

Careers in Public Health

Anyone interested in helping people or doing detective work should consider a career in public health. Public health professionals find satisfaction in working to improve life for people who live in their communities. Public health is a discipline that can be applied in almost any place in the world. In fact, many countries desperately need public health workers.

Who They Are

Many public health workers are scientists, doctors, and educators. Public health can use people with many other talents as well. For example, an engineer might work to design safer roadways or a better type of water treatment plant. That engineer is contributing to the health of a community.

In the field of medicine, public health is a recognized specialty. Some doctors have advanced training in public health in much the same way that surgeons and psychiatrists have advanced, highly specialized training. It is common for a physician to head a public health team.

Epidemiologists are scientists who specialize in solving health mysteries. Their work has become more important than ever, now that strange new diseases are emerging, such as Ebola virus. As human beings encroach upon the rain forests and other important wildlife habitats, diseases are moving from creatures of the wild to become deadly threats to humans. In the age of airline travel, diseases have an effective new way to spread widely and quickly throughout the world.

Where They Work

Many public health specialists are employed in hospitals, universities, and private industry. Others work in consulting and research.

Public health officials are employed at all levels of government. In local communities, sanitarians and health officers ensure that establishments handle food safely. They enforce local regulations so that communities can stay safe and healthy. The requirements for these positions vary from state to state. A career sanitarian usually has some college education; health officers must have experience and, often, an advanced degree.

> The Public Health Service Commissioned Corps employs approximately 6,000 professionals, including dentists, pharmacists, physicians, dietitians, veterinarians, scientists, nurses, therapists, engineers, environmental health experts, and health service workers (social workers, physician assistants, optometrists, statisticians, computer scientists, dental hygienists, and medical records administrators, among others). See the resources section for more information.

Nationally, many government agencies are involved in public health, including the departments of Agriculture, Commerce, Health and Human Services (including the CDC and PHS Commissioned Corps), Labor, Transportation, and Veterans Affairs. All of the armed forces have professionals to help maintain the health of their members and prevent injuries.

Internationally, the opportunities to apply public health skills are almost unlimited. Basic services such as sanitation and clean water are unavailable to many people in the world. Bringing good public health measures such as education, immunizations, and medications to communities worldwide could greatly reduce suffering and deaths from disease.

Volunteer agencies also employ public health professionals. The American Red Cross helps in disasters. The American Heart Association, American Cancer Association, and American Lung Association are a few other organizations that employ public health professionals.

Qualifications

Public health officials often are active people who get a sense of satisfaction from helping others or doing something worthwhile. These are important traits for a public health career because many positions include travel and assisting people as part of the usual routine. Most professional careers in public health require specialized education with a college degree as a minimum requirement. Areas of study may include chemistry, biology, engineering, mathematics, and psychology, as well as policy formulation, finance, economics, and marketing. Business and law experience can be useful to a person wanting to serve as a public health professional.

Good sources of information about the field of public health are your merit badge counselor, school guidance counselor, library, local health department, or science teacher, or a practicing public health professional. Scholarships and other programs are available to help qualified young people enter the field of public health.

Resources

Scouting Literature

Boy Scout Handbook; Fieldbook; Animal Science, Camping, Citizenship in the Community, Citizenship in the Nation, Citizenship in the World, Cooking, Dentistry, Emergency Preparedness, Environmental Science, First Aid, Medicine, Safety, and *Soil and Water Conservation* merit badge pamphlets

For more information about Scouting-related resources, visit the BSA's online retail catalog (with your parent's permission) at *http://www.scoutstuff.org.*

Books

Altman, Linda Jacobs. *Plague and Pestilence: A History of Infectious Disease.* Enslow, 1998.

American Medical Association. *Health Care Almanac: Every Person's Guide to the Thoughtful and Practical Sides of Medicine.* American Medical Association, 1998.

Friedlander, Mark P. *Outbreak: Disease Detectives at Work.* Lerner, 2000.

Giblin, James. *When Plague Strikes: The Black Death, Smallpox, AIDS.* HarperCollins, 1995.

Gittleman, Anne Louise. *Guess What Came to Dinner? Parasites and Your Health.* Avery, 2001.

Grant, Pamela. *Water.* Thameside Press, 2000.

Marrin, Albert. *Dr. Jenner and the Speckled Monster: The Search for the Smallpox Vaccine.* Dutton, 2002.

Nardo, Don. *Vaccines.* Lucent, 2001.

Pickett, George E. *Opportunities in Public Health Careers.* VGM Career Horizons, 1995.

Stewart, Gail. *Teens With Cancer.* Lucent, 2001.

White, Katherine. *Everything You Need to Know About AIDS and HIV.* Rosen, 2001.

Yount, Lisa. *Disease Detectives.* Lucent, 2001.

Organizations and Web Sites

Centers for Disease Control and Prevention
1600 Clifton Road
Atlanta, GA 30333
Toll-free telephone: 800-311-3435
Web site: *http://www.cdc.gov*

Environmental Protection Agency
Ariel Rios Building
1200 Pennsylvania Ave. NW
Washington, DC 20460
Telephone: 202-272-0167
Web site: *http://www.epa.gov*

National Institutes of Health
9000 Rockville Pike
Bethesda, MD 20892
Telephone: 301-496-4000
Web site: *http://www.nih.gov*

U.S. Department of Health and Human Services
Office of Disease Prevention and Health Promotion
1101 Wootton Parkway, Suite LL100
Rockville, MD 20852
Telephone: 240-453-8280
Web site: *http://odphp.osophs.dhhs.gov*

U.S. Public Health Service Commissioned Corps
1101 Wootton Parkway, Suite LL100
Rockville, MD 20852
Toll-free telephone: 800-279-1605
Web site: *http://www.usphs.gov*

U.S. Department of Health and Human Services
200 Independence Ave. SW
Washington, DC 20201
Telephone: 202-619-0257
Web site: *http://www.hhs.gov*

World Health Organization
Web site: *http://www.who.int*

Acknowledgments

The Boy Scouts of America is thankful to the following subject experts for their assistance with this new edition of the *Public Health* merit badge pamphlet: Eric J. Pyle, Ph.D., Department of Education Theory and Practice, West Virginia University; Gerald F. Pyle, Ph.D., Department of Health Promotions and Kinesiology, University of North Carolina–Charlotte; and Richard W. Klomp, Information Management Team, Centers for Disease Control and Prevention.

Thanks to the Centers for Disease Control and Prevention, Atlanta, Georgia, for providing the information found in the "Recommended Childhood and Adolescent Immunization Schedule."

Photo and Illustration Credits

Centers for Disease Control and Prevention—pages 9 and 13

©2001 Comstock Inc.—page 48

©Jupiterimages.com—cover *(eye chart, ambulance)*

National Safety Council—page 58

Natural Resources Conservation Service, courtesy—page 65

©Photos.com—cover *(washing hands, syringes, water bottles, trash cans, sharps container);* pages 6, 20, 36, 38 *(background),* 46 *(all),* 49, 60, 62, 67–68 *(both),* and 73–74 *(all)*

USDA Agricultural Research Service, courtesy—cover *(mosquito);* pages 16 and 37

U.S. Department of Agriculture, courtesy—page 41

All other photos and illustrations not mentioned above are the property of or are protected by the Boy Scouts of America.

BSA Risk Management—page 71

Dan Bryant—pages 24–25 *(both),* 51, and 54

Daniel Giles—pages 8, 19, 23, 26, 29–32 (all), 53, 57, 64, and 66

John McDearmon—pages 38 *(tick illustrations),* 59, and 63

Steve Seeger—page 40